The Dance of Bullying

The Dance of Bullying

A Breakthrough Tool
for
Teachers and Parents

Kenneth L. Pierce and Alice M. Taylor

The Dance of Bullying
A Breakthrough Tool for Teachers and Parents

iUniverse books may be ordered through booksellers or by contacting:

iUniverse
1663 Liberty Drive
Bloomington, IN 47403
www.iuniverse.com
844-349-9409

ISBN: 978-0-5954-5303-0 (sc)
ISBN: 978-0-5957-0156-8 (hc)
ISBN: 978-0-5958-9616-5 (e)

Print information available on the last page.

iUniverse rev. date: 05/04/2023

This is dedicated to my love and life partner, F. Anna Pierce.
—Ken Pierce

I dedicate this book to all teachers and parents who would love to see children evolve from "victim and/or perpetrator" to balance, through the power of gratitude and unconditional love.
—Alice Taylor

So divinely is the world organized that every one of us, in our place and time, is in balance with everything.

—Johann Wolfgang von Goethe

I am what I am both as a result of people who respected me and helped me, and of those who did not respect me and treated me badly.

—Nelson Mandela

Contents

List of Figures and Tables

Acknowledgements

While one or a few people may write a book, it takes many to create it. Like others before us, we have a list of people to whom we own a debt of gratitude for inspiring us in some form to take on the joy and pain of writing.

Ken would like to express his gratitude to the following people:

Alice, my colleague and friend, who suggested we do this and persisted against many obstacles, besides me, to make it happen.

My students and seminar participants over the years who graciously considered the ideas I collected and helped me explore them, and evolve in ways I could not have imagined.

Christina Gaudet for her creativity and professionalism in illustrating our work, as well as, my daughter Stephanie, who took the time to draw some cartoons and review an early manuscript.

And, especially my family: Anna, my spouse, who is a constant and stable source of support and challenge to everything I do; my three wonder-filled daughters, Michele, Stephanie and Leanna, who keep me grounded with their affection and humour; and Hunter, my first grandchild, who doesn't know or care about what I do, he just loves me.

Alice would like to express her gratitude to the following people:

My colleague and friend, Ken, who by supporting and challenging me kept me focused on the task at hand of getting the manuscript to print.

The parents who gave their permission to use their children's stories as a way of assisting others to understand the concepts presented in this book.

My niece, Lola Honeybone, whose critique and poignant feedback served as a catalyst for us to clarify our thinking and our writing.

My students, who through the years have graciously received each "new" theory in my attempt to find "the right match" for each of them so as to propel their learning, as well as my own.

My family: my three sons Donald, David and Stephen, and my daughters-in-law Terri-Jane and Janina, whose courage and ability to stand in the centre of the fire of life and not look back inspires me; their beautiful children, my grandchildren, Aleigha, Ryan, McKenna, Kaylen, Chad, Olivia and Noah who, each in their own unique way, have blessed me on my journey into the heart of love and helped me find gratitude and true fulfillment.

And *most profoundly*, my husband Wayne, my soul mate, whose love is manifest in countless ways, most particularly in his unwavering patience, understanding and appreciation for me just as I am.

Ken & Alice's Special Acknowledgement

We wish to express a special thank you to Dr. John F. Demartini and Dr. William Glasser.

John Demartini, inventor of the ground breaking Demartini Method®—formerly called The Quantum Collapse Process®—and founder of the Demartini Human Research and Education Foundation, is a pioneer on the frontiers of human consciousness. We have been fortunate to have experienced several of his leading-edge programs. Without John's work and our exposure to it this book would not have emerged.

William Glasser, creator of Choice Theory©, Reality Therapy, and Lead Management is a world leader in understanding human motivation, needs and behaviour. His renowned ideas and approach have impacted many areas of the human condition and his principles have become a way of approaching life for many. His work served as a catalyst for this book and our own evolution.

We are grateful for the opportunities we have had to work with Dr. Demartini and Dr. Glasser's principles, tools and techniques.

Foreword

Bullying continues to be a focus of public attention both in our educational environments and in our communities at large. Yet this topic has not been fully addressed in a way that allows us to understand the underlying social dynamic that is unfolding before us. There has been little attention given to how it both costs and benefits us as a species and as a society. *The Dance of Bullying ... A Breakthrough Tool for Teachers and Parents* addresses this succinctly.

Using two of nature's fundamental laws, conservation and symmetry, this book offers the reader a deeper and fuller understanding of how bullying functions in the human social dynamic. It is indeed a new look during a time when a fresh perspective is warranted. It incorporates the latest research, ideas and tools available.

The authors, Ken Pierce and Alice Taylor, have developed an insightful and pragmatic approach to this important topic. I am inspired to see how they have incorporated the innovative Demartini Method—formerly called The Quantum Collapse Process—into their most significant approach.

Ken, a registered psychologist and experienced corporate trainer, and Alice, a seasoned educator and life coach, have extensive experience utilizing the Demartini Method in a variety of interpersonal applications. I applaud their initiative since my own work has demonstrated to me over the years the value and impact of approaching the human condition from such a sound scientific foundation.

What you hold in your hands is a new, inspired and practical work. I am confident you will be as impressed as I am. *The Dance of Bullying ... A Breakthrough Tool for Teachers and Parents* is a lovely book! It is clear and concise on principles and practices. I am inspired by the applications this work will have on society's approach to schoolyard bullying. With the well-illustrated text and detailed description of the Demartini Method, you will be well-prepared to evolve your own thinking and approach to schoolyard bullying. The key points that are highlighted and the chapter summaries make it easy to get at the crux of the material. And the workbook in the appendices offers specific techniques for integration in the classroom or at home.

I invite you to use *The Dance of Bullying ... A Breakthrough Tool for Teachers and Parents* and see for yourself how it will assist you in your work.

Dr. John F. Demartini
Founder of the Demartini Human Research and Education Foundation and best-selling author of *The Breakthrough Experience—A Revolutionary Approach to Personal Transformation*

Introduction

Bullying is not a new behaviour in our society or indeed our schools. However, reporting of it seems to be more prevalent and its impact appears to be more dramatic. Is it really more prevalent or are we unwittingly fostering it with our current approaches?

The Dance of Bullying … A Breakthrough Tool for Teachers and Parents is an entirely new look at the bullying event from a perspective that is both insightful and pragmatic. This perspective draws on not just the fields of education and psychology but also other scientific disciplines. We have known for some time that there is a human dynamic going on between the bully and the bullied. We have also known for some time that it is often the same specific children who are involved in such incidents. *The Dance of Bullying … A Breakthrough Tool for Teachers and Parents* explains why this is so, what is going on and how to intervene. *The Dance of Bullying … A Breakthrough Tool for Teachers and Parents* provides the reader with both a strategy and training paradigm for interventions.

The Dance of Bullying … A Breakthrough Tool for Teachers and Parents is written for teachers and educational administrators, those called upon to deal directly with the phenomenon of bullying on a regular basis. It is directed primarily at those who work in middle Schools, grades three through nine. However, it can be adapted to any educational or workplace environment. *The Dance of Bullying … A Breakthrough Tool for Teachers and Parents* also addresses the concerns of parents in a special chapter.

The Dance of Bullying … A Breakthrough Tool for Teachers and Parents demonstrate that the two parties in those events are actually attracted to each other by forces of nature that demand that they each learn important life lessons. The bullied needs to learn more respect for self and the bully needs to learn more respect for others. It is this mutual need to learn from each other that draws them together. It is not a conscious process and yet is a powerful one, since it reflects two of the most pervasive and powerful laws of nature, those of conservation and symmetry.

The Dance of Bullying … A Breakthrough Tool for Teachers and Parents, will help readers develop a deeper understanding of the bullying phenomenon so that they can intervene in a way that facilitates the evolution of both parties in this dance. As well, a training session is available which will enable interveners to learn and practice these ideas in ways that ensure that children evolve in useful ways from these experiences.

The Dance of Bullying ... A Breakthrough Tool for Teachers and Parents has been carefully designed to appeal to the busy professional. It aims for simplicity and clarity. It defines chapter goals, provides examples and illustrations, highlights important points and summarizes each chapter. In addition, appendix 4 includes activities to help teachers and others to utilize the ideas with students. Finally, it provides the reader with direct access to the authors for any questions or follow-up required.

Preface

The phenomenon of bullying has been receiving wide-spread attention over the past number of years, exaggerated by a few violent mass slayings that somehow have been connected rather arbitrarily to the perpetrators being bullying victims. At the same time, we have yet to find anyone who has not experienced some form of bullying or who has not been viewed by others as being a bully. So is bullying a new behaviour recently acquired to deal with modern life, or just an old behaviour that has been around for a long time and actually serves some purpose in human evolution?

During our 60-plus years of experience in psychology and education, we have had occasion to deal with many forms of bullying that arose with children from two to 22 years of age. As we looked back, in each case there was invariably significant, specific, individualized learning for each person in the event, whether it was the bully, the bullied, the observer or the intervener. It suggested to us that bullying is a tool that we all use to evolve as individuals. It suggested that bullying is a tool that we all use to learn important things about ourselves, other people and the world in general. It suggested that bullying is a behaviour we all use in various forms.

Our own professional work has been to: first, help students to appreciate where they have come from—their family, their culture, and their community; second, to honour with gratitude who they are now; and third, to encourage them to bring their unique talents, presence and certainty to their future.

To assist learners in this journey we have utilized cutting-edge strategies from the fields of education and psychology. These had some degree of success. But still there were questions and gaps, so our quest continued. Our most recent focus has been in the area of psycho-physics and the pioneering work of Dr. John Demartini, where the natural laws that govern our universe, as described in such sciences as physics, biology, chemistry and cosmology, are being applied to human perceptions, relationships, systems and evolution. It is fascinating, ground-breaking work.

Meanwhile, vast amounts of resources are being devoted to addressing bullying at the public school level, where it is hoped it can be stopped in its tracks. As we read about yet another program focused at some group of youth in the community, we wondered if perhaps all this attention was actually adding confusion rather than clarity to the situation. We wondered if perhaps a rational, scientific and experienced perspective would be valuable in addressing the concerns of our community on this issue. This is our response to that question.

Utilizing the work of Dr. John Demartini and Dr. William Glasser, we have treated bullying as an evolutionary social tool that has always been and will be part of the behaviour repertoire of humankind. We offer you here a fuller understanding of bullying, its role in learning environments and how to intervene. To accelerate your learning we have highlighted the main ideas, concluded chapters with "Seven Key Chapter Points" and offered both additional Demartini Method instructions and "Learning Activities for the Classroom and Home." in the Appendices

Chapter One

A New Approach to Bullying

Life is not the way it is supposed to be; it is the way it is.
The way you cope with it is what makes the difference.

—Virginia Satir

The Genesis of the Dance

These two teachers are expressing the thoughts of many individuals, parents, educators and community leaders. Bullying in all of its forms seems to be on the rise. It seems to be taking on unique and bizarre forms.

Richard Feynman, considered by many as Albert Einstein's successor, believed that if all scientific knowledge was destroyed and if only one statement was passed on the next generation, it should be the atomic hypothesis "that all things are made of atoms."[1]

As a species we have acknowledged for some time that there are universal laws or rules that pervade and govern our world's atomic nature. The pure sciences of physics, chemistry, biology, geology, astronomy and cosmology acknowledge this and are intent on uncovering these universal laws. But we have been less aware that humans are part of the natural world. As such we are also made of atoms and so are equally governed by the same universal laws. Knowing the essential atomic nature of ones own essence and its implications opens a student up to the new possibilities of learning and life. This is especially so with the bullying events of our lives. This awareness enables them to live life more fully from the inside out. Imagine what it would be like to have this knowledge through childhood, into adolescence and beyond.

> **As such we are also made of atoms and so are equally governed by the same universal laws.**

Join us now in our goal of explaining how the laws of nature offer both insight and practical methods for addressing bullying. For the purposes of this book we shall focus our attention on the forms of bullying that take place with children between the ages of 8 and 14 years.

The Definitions of the Dance Participants

In figure 1.1, we see all the players in the dance. The very language we use to describe it exemplifies our perceptions of bullying events.

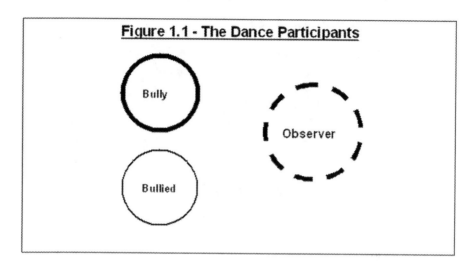

Figure 1.1 - The Dance Participants

Let's consider how it is defined.

What is a *bully*?

The Concise Oxford English Dictionary describes a bully as: "a person who deliberately intimidates or persecutes those who are weaker"

What is a *bullied*?

This word is in the Concise Oxford English Dictionary only as a verb not as a noun. Since the bullied person is often thought of as the victim, let's check for it. This dictionary describes a victim as: "a person who has come to feel helpless and passive in the face of misfortune."

Please note: We will use the term "bullied" as a verb but also at times as a noun when referring to this person in the bully dance; the person often termed the victim.

What is an *observer*?

Frequently there is a third party in the dance—the observer. So let's check the Oxford dictionary again for the meaning of observer. "Observer: one who examines and notes phenomenon without aid of experiment."

What is *evolution*?

And the Concise Oxford English Dictionary defines it as "the process by which different kinds of living organisms are believed to have developed from earlier forms." So we will use the term evolve in this work to describe how humans "develop gradually" using the behaviour of bullying.

What is different about this book?

Schoolyard bullying, the focus of this work, is perhaps one of the least-understood child interactions in modern society. As a social phenomenon, its study only began in the early 1970s with the work of a Norwegian, Dan Olweus and his 1978 book, *Aggression in the Schools—Bullying and Whipping Boys,* Olweus's definition of bullying has become somewhat of a standard: "A person is being bullied when he or she is exposed, repeatedly and over time, to negative actions on the part of one or more persons."[2]

Early research focused on the more direct forms of verbal and physical bullying, including punching, kicking, vandalizing, gesturing and making faces. More recently, research has been expanded to include new, indirect forms, including gossiping, spreading rumours, social exclusion and other acts intent on damaging relationships. The emergence of electronic communication devices has added new forms of bullying.

Since Olweus's initial work, social bullying has also been studied in England, Australia, Zimbabwe, the United States and Canada. Some of the recent research findings of special interest to our approach include the following.

Roxie Alcaraz at the University of California points out that while bullying in American schools is not a new phenomenon and was accepted as a normal part of growing up; due to media attention after several school shootings; it has been projected to the forefront of public scrutiny. She notes, "Educators, parents, communities, and policy makers have responded to bullying and its possible detrimental outcomes with increased attention to the causes and impact of bullying behaviour and with implementation of innovative anti-bullying programs across the country."[3]

A longitudinal study by Pellegrini and Long found that generally bullying and aggression increased with the transition to middle school and then declined. As well, they suggest that "bullying may be one way in which young adolescents manage peer and dominance relationships as they make the transition in to new social groups." Interestingly, they note also that victimization was counterbalanced by "peer affiliation."[4]

Foreshadowing this book's theme and ideas, Bauman, Sheri, Hurley and Cindy, in their work on teachers' attitudes and beliefs about bullying, found that "some teachers hold beliefs that are at odds with current best practices in bullying prevention and intervention."[5]

Finally, as Craig, Peters and Konarski point out in their work, bullying and victimization are relatively new areas of research and what has been done to date has been mostly looking at the rate of occurrence, where, when and by whom. "As a result, the field is lacking theoretical models of bullying and victimization behaviour."[6] Very little has been done to provide a theoretical analysis of why it occurs. Some developmental theorists perceive bullying as a child's attempt to establish social dominance over other children, while social theorists posit that bullying occurs as a result of a power differential between different groups in society, mainly different genders, races or ethnicities, or different social classes.

While the research has been useful, it has tended to take a traditional view of psychology and human development. It does not take into account the perspective of considering bullying as applications of established scientific principles found in other fields, most notably, physics. As a result, it does not reflect the latest scientific knowledge, models, or tools to deal with bullying on a practical level. Our work will take a unique approach, incorporating some of the latest paradigms from the field of physics, which heretofore has not been viewed as having any significant contribution to make.

> **It does not take into account the perspective of considering bullying as applications of established scientific principles found in other fields, most notably, physics.**

Frequency of Bullying

The phenomenon of bullying has a long history and yet only recently came into the limelight as a focus of study and resource allocation. Our history books and news media are filled with tales of bullying. An overview of the literature suggests wide ranges of both bullying and victimization from three per cent to 66 per cent.

Johnson reports that The National Institute of Child Health and Human Development estimated that 1.6 million children in grades six through 10 were affected by weekly bullying in the United States; that approximately 75 per cent of bullying is unobserved or ignored by teachers; that a majority of bullying episodes occurred when students were involved in solitary, unsupervised tasks; and that half of bullied pupils will not tell teachers or parents because of fear, embarrassment, or concerns that nothing will be done.[7]

In Canada, Craig et al. report about one in seven boys between the ages of four and 11 (14 per cent) bully others and approximately one in 20 (five per cent) are victimized by others sometimes or very often. Approximately one in 11 girls between the ages of four and 11 (nine per cent) bully others, while one in 14 are victimized (seven per cent). For both boys and girls, however, victimization increased with age. At all ages, there were a higher percentage of boys compared to girls involved in bullying.[8]

The authors point out that these figures are comparable to other countries, including both Norway and Great Britain, and go on to speak to the urgency of the situation. "The prevalence of bullying and victimization in Canada highlights the need to design and implement effective interaction programs."[9] As well, Craig et al. note that there are very few victimized children who are not aggressive themselves and that stress (i.e., low income, unemployment, lack of education) within the family may promote bullying and victimizing behaviours among the children.[10]

Findings like these certainly add to our understanding of bullying and offer us ideas as to how it emerges, but do little to direct us towards assisting those who experience bullying to move beyond it. What we know for sure is that, as a human behaviour, bullying has always been with us in one form or another.

The Nature of Bullying

Each "ology" we consider, such as geology, cosmology, biology, psychology, sociology, etc., has the same fundamental purpose, namely, to understand some aspect of how nature operates and to seek out some universal law or principle that will explain what we are observing. In other words, to answer the question: "What are nature's overriding principles or laws that prevail throughout the universe?" It was Albert Einstein's dream to discover a unified theory that would explain both classical and particle physics. Einstein wanted to uncover the laws that apply to sub-atomic particles and star systems. At a fundamental level, this has been and continues to be the goal of all science: to understand the basic laws that describe all aspects of the natural world.

Richard Feynman said that the most important hypothesis in biology today is to prove that everything that animals do, atoms also do, regardless of what it might be. "In other words, there is nothing that living things do that cannot be understood according to the laws of physics."[11] Or to put it another way, "All things are made of atoms, and ... everything that living things do can be understood in terms of the jigglings and wigglings of atoms."[12] In its efforts to achieve this worthy goal, science has uncovered many laws of nature that apply across the entire universe. Two of these are the laws of symmetry and conservation.

The Laws of Symmetry and Conservation

Friedrich Nietzsche said that we must be physicists in order to be creative since our codes of values and ideals have been constructed in ignorance of physics, or even in contradiction to our knowledge of physics. Perhaps bullying is not a bad thing or even a good thing but rather an application of physics that we have not understood before. What is *not* being noticed is that schoolyard bullying, in all of its forms, is actually a demonstration or dramatization of two primary laws of physics: the law of symmetry and the law of conservation. These two laws are expressed at every level of existence throughout nature.

The law of symmetry states that every part of the universe is in a continual state of equilibrium, balance or symmetry. This law of symmetry has been proven to be true within and between atoms as well as, at the levels of molecules, cells, organs, bodily systems, relationships, families, organizations, communities, planets, constellations, galaxies, galaxy clusters, etc.

The law of conservation states that energy and matter are never consumed but only change in form and that the total energy in any system is constant and cannot be increased or decreased.

Put simply, Einstein proved that matter and energy are constant in the universe and that our universe is in a constant state of perfect balance. Logically, then, every relationship and event, including school yard bullying, has symmetry to it and must also be a balanced event in the universe. So, if we adopt the perception that school yard bullying is primarily a negative event then we are missing the counterbalancing positive events that must also be occurring.

So, from the field of physics we can learn three things that warrant our attention:

- First, that all events in the universe are balanced events, including schoolyard bullying, to comply with the law of symmetry

- Second, that schoolyard bullying, to comply with the underlying law of conservation of energy and matter, has both a negative and positive component

- Third, that schoolyard bullying has not only both a positive and negative impact but that also these effects are in an equal and perfect balance to each other to comply with the law of symmetry

---

What is often not noticed is that "school bullying" is actually a demonstration of two of these primary laws of nature, the laws of symmetry and of conservation.

Brian Greene, a professor of physics and mathematics at Columbia University, in his acclaimed best-seller *The Elegant Universe,* reiterates the same point about symmetry's part in every aspect of nature, including human perception: "nature treats every moment in time and every location in space identically—symmetrically—by ensuring that the same fundamental laws are in operation."[13]

How does this occur in relationships?

Leon Lederman, Nobel Prize wining physicist, illuminates the law of symmetry in human relationships when he notes in his best-selling work *The God Particle,* "We first encounter symmetries in our experiences as children. We see them, we hear them, and we experience situations and events that seem to have certain symmetrical interrelationships."[14]

As young children, we see how water always seeks it own balance or symmetry. We observe how the seasons balance each other on the earth. We notice how each day is balanced by the night. Think of your own family: did you experience one parent assuming the role of being supportive while the other was challenging? And interestingly, when the roles switched and the challenger became supportive did you see the supporter become more challenging?

Parents create the counterbalance for each other. With single-parent families the same symmetry applies, with someone else in the child's life providing the symmetrical opposite, either challenge or support, to that of the primary parental figure. Perhaps it is a sibling, aunt, uncle, grandparent, or even a friend or neighbour. We might even remember incidents when a teacher challenged us; it was invariably accompanied by someone in our life who supported us.

As adults, we often start noticing that our stable relationships are characterized by not just the similarities but equally by the differences. You might have noticed, for example, that it takes the symmetry of an optimist and a pessimist combined to create a strong and healthy relationship, whether with a spouse or friend. As we grow older, we find more and more varied and personal examples of this symmetry in more parts of our life.

> **You might have noticed that it takes the symmetry of an optimist and a pessimist combined to create a strong and healthy relationship, whether with a spouse or friend.**

The Symmetry of Bullying—An Example

Let's apply this law of symmetry to the dance of bullying.

When we consider a generic bullying situation, the bullying person often displays traits like independence and high self-confidence, which can be characterized as projecting a positive emotional charge. At the same time, the bullied person displays traits such as dependence and low self-confidence, which project a negative emotional charge. At extreme levels they are sometimes termed elation and depression.

Since within the laws of physics, as demonstrated in electricity and magnets, positively and negatively charged particles (including people who are emotionally charged) attract each other, then this would suggest that the two people actually attract each other in order for each to play their part in a natural balancing phenomenon.[15]

So, for example, one could say that the bully has too much of a positive charge on these two traits (independence, self-confidence) while the bullied has too little of a charge on the same traits. When they interact, they each draw from the other and they each come closer to balance on these traits. Considering the trait of independence as an example, the bully is too independent while the bullied is too dependent, while with regard to the trait of confidence, the bully displays too much self-confidence while the bullied displays too little self-confidence.

> **… then this would suggest that the two people actually attract each other in order for each to play their part in a natural balancing phenomenon.**

We add emotionally-charged language to describe these traits:

- Too independent is often described as "arrogant," "cold," "aggressive"
- Too assertive is often described as "demanding," "mean," "unkind"
- Too confident is often described as "disrespectful," "cruel," "stupid"
- Too dependent is often described as "fragile," "fearful," "needy"
- Too passive is often described as "soft," "afraid," "submissive"
- Too unconfident is often described as "apprehensive," "inexperienced," "humble"

These polarities in our language are what continually demonstrate the duality of these two dance partners. Consider the two dance partners as described in figure 1.2, before they meet in the event.

Figure 1.2 - The Two Dance Partners before the Exchange

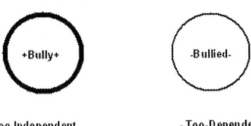

+Bully+

+ Too-Independent
+ Too- Assertive
+ Too-Confident

-Bullied-

- Too-Dependent
- Too-Passive
- Too-Unconfident

As outlined in figure 1.2, before the dance begins the bullying person, as excessively positively charged (+), will exhibit too much independence, assertiveness and confidence. At the same time, the bullied person, as excessively negatively charged (-), will exhibit the opposite traits of not enough independence, assertiveness or confidence, which is also termed too dependent, too passive and too unconfident. In figure 1.3, we see how imbalanced they are in relation to each other. So the bully has an excess of these traits and the bullied has a deficit of the same traits.

Since the law of conservation says that energy and matter cannot be created or destroyed, only changed in form, so the bully and bullied do not eliminate their charged states but rather exchange their charged states to maintain the balanced system in keeping with the law of symmetry. In so doing, they actually exchange energy, which is also what we call information or learning. In figure 1.4, we see how they have come to balance from their previous states.

So, according to the laws of conservation and symmetry, these two people move toward each other implicitly and unconsciously in order to balance the energy or emotional charges they are carrying.

To put it in lay terms, an arrogant, mean and disrespectful bully and a needy, submissive and humble victim will unconsciously and implicitly be attracted toward each other in the same way that the north and south poles of two bar magnets are attracted to each other. It is a law of nature, if you will, a law of physics and what we term "science."

> **In so doing, they actually exchange energy, which is also what we call information or learning.**

So, from the perspective of psycho-physics, the dance and the exchange of energy or information can be expressed as: the bully learns from the bullied to be less independent, less assertive and less confident, while the bullied learns from the bully to be more independent, more assertive and more confident. So they exchange energy (ionic charges), which is, simply put, information. And so both then are essential to the balance of the system.

Figure 1.3 - The Two Dance Partners During the Exchange

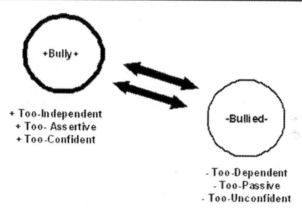

Figure 1.4 - The Two Dance Partners after the Exchange

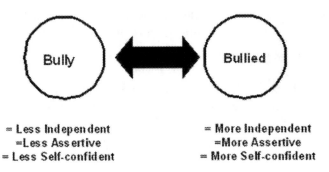

Bully	Bullied
= Less Independent	= More Independent
=Less Assertive	=More Assertive
= Less Self-confident	= More Self-confident

When bullying is viewed in this manner, it enables one to see it as a learning tool for the evolution of the people involved. And it is not just a tool for the two people who are engaged in the experience but also for others who are involved on the periphery. Anyone observing the bully dance, such as an educator, also can carry a positive, negative or balanced charge. Depending on their charge, they will either contribute toward the re-establishment of a balance or contribute toward an imbalance. Thus, the educator's role is a vital one. It is this role that this book addresses. Using the ideas and techniques found in *The Dance of Bullying ... A Breakthrough Tool for Teachers and Parents* enables the educator to intervene in a way that restores balance to the relationships. This is the purpose of this book.

> **Using the ideas and techniques found in *The Dance of Bullying ... A Breakthrough Tool for Teachers and Parents* enables the educator to intervene in a way that restores balance to the relationships.**

Let's follow Alice through two examples.
Example 1—Mary Ann
    Mary Ann, age 12, complained of having no friends at school. She told stories of how people in her class teased her about her clothes, her hair and her general appearance. They ignored her at recess and lunchtime and made her bus rides so unpleasant her parents succumbed to the pressure and drove her to and from

school. Mary Ann was frequently ill with stomach aches, nausea and other such stress-related illnesses. She missed many days from school. In fact, she did not want to go to school at all and was begging her parents for home schooling.

In an effort to make life a little more bearable, her parents moved her from one school to another. As well, they encouraged her to pursue her interest in horses, where she felt comfortable, confident and unthreatened. She readily interacted with her horses and other animals without fear of rejection or ridicule. Here, she found a safe environment. However, many of her challenges in other parts of her life remained the same.

Mary Ann was displaying many of the traits associated with being bullied and being a partner in a bully dance. She was very dependent on her parents to solve her challenges, particularly in school. She tended to withdraw under the verbal attacks of her school mates. She had little confidence in herself or her abilities. Mary Ann was also into a mind set where she tended to think that others "*always*" treated her with ridicule and distain, or that "*no one*" ever paid "*any*" attention to her or included her in "*anything*". Sometimes her parents felt exasperated because they had a strong desire to see their daughter shine in all parts of her life. They also wisely understood their child needed some assistance.

As I got to know Mary Ann she shared her story. While listening to her perception of the situation it became clear there was a dance at play here. Mary Ann was displaying the classic characteristics of a bullied child and she perceived herself as a "victim of bullying" at school.

So our work began. With a little prodding, Mary Ann identified how being bullied was a drawback to her at school. Since it was all she could think about, she acknowledged it was a situation that was literally running her life. My task was to help Mary Ann see the balance in this situation, so we looked at how being bullied was actually also a benefit to her. At first she was very sceptical. But as she worked at it she began to realize, slowly at first, the benefits that were there and how they actually equalled the losses.

Since the same laws of conservation and symmetry that apply in nature apply within each person, I knew that what we see outside is just a counterbalance or reflection of what is on the inside. As a result, it was clear that she was attracting this bullying situation to help her know and appreciate a part of herself she had not yet owned and valued.

So I asked this question: "Mary Ann, where are you a bully?" She replied indignantly, "I am not a bully!" Once she recovered from the question we explored other parts of her life. With some prodding she realized that when friends came to her home to play she became quite bossy and possessive, especially when they were around her beloved horses and other animals. In fact, she looked at them with some distain for their lack of know-how in caring for and interacting with animals. As difficult as it was for her, she did acknowledge she was bullying as well. And she eventually understood that it likely played a role in her not having many friends.

I remember her face at the moment she realized that she too used bullying behaviours and that some very specific people viewed her as a bully. Added to this was her realization that in fact her behaviours were very similar in nature to the behaviours of her school mates she complained about so vigorously. It was one of those "Eureka!" moments that changed how she looked at her school mates and especially herself. She saw in herself the behaviours of her bullying classmates: too independent, too assertive and too confident. The only difference was her bullying behaviours took place around her beloved horses, a place where she had developed much confidence and competence.

From here it was not long before we were discussing how to build and maintain friendships. We identified areas of her life, both inside and outside of school, where she chose to build more independence, where she desired to actively assert herself and where she would practice building her self-confidence.

Since that time, Mary Ann has attracted and kept friends. There are not a lot of them but there are several who have stuck with her through "good times and bad." She will graduate next year from her high school. Mary Ann utilized her learning from her bullying dance outside of school as well. It is interesting how this young woman was able to make the connection between her love of horses and school. She continues to develop her expertise with horses; this focus on her life's purpose also keeps her in school as she connects her high school graduation with her burning desire to pursue a career as an accomplished horsewoman. Mary Ann has practiced some of her newfound applications of assertiveness by spending several weeks out of country last year honing her horsemanship. School became a means to an end as she saw the knowledge and skills she was developing as necessary to fulfill her dream, that of enabling her to do what she loves.

At the writing of this book, Mary Ann is a 17-year-old who has clearly articulated ambitions to become a leading horsewoman. She plans to own her own ranch, raise horses, compete throughout North America and teach others all she knows about horses and their care. With her independent, assertive planning, her commitment and dedication to her goals, and her self-confident manner, it is highly likely she will achieve her dreams.

Let's take a look at the specifics of Mary Ann's work (See table 1.1) from seven perspectives that cover the range of human outlooks: spiritual, mental, vocational, financial, social, familial, and physical.[16] What were the gains and losses of being "bullied" for Mary Ann?

Table 1.1 - MaryAnn's Gains & Losses		
7 Areas of Life	**+ Gains +**	**- Losses -**
Spiritual Inner Voice; Sense of Purpose; Vital Spark	+ Gained the ability to listen clearly to her inner voice.	- Lost some of her vital spark.
Mental Self-Esteem, Self-Confidence, Mental Acuity	+ Gained some self esteem in new areas of her life.	- Lost some of her self-confidence in social areas of her life.
Vocational Education, Career, Purposeful Work	+ Gained for her purposeful work and a potential career.	- Lost sight of her other educational goals.
Financial Wealth, Managing Resources; Self-Worth	+ Gained in self worth in new areas of her life.	- Lost valuable resources like learning, opportunities and time.
Familial Connectedness; Family Relationships, Harmony	+ Gained new connections to family support.	- Lost closeness with some individual family members.
Social Friends, Colleagues Circle of influence	+ Gained skills in making and keeping friends.	- Lost other potential relationships in the larger community.
Physical Energy, Wellness, Health	+ Gained stamina and vitality in new areas of life.	- Lost balance and wellness.

As we look at Mary Ann's gains and losses in her life, we can see her desire to be in the "horse world" exclusively, where she felt safe, was at the expense of her school world where she felt unsafe. As we look underneath the events in her life we can see that the bully dance in which she was engaged assisted her to evolve from this situation and to learn priceless skills that will be useful throughout her life.

It also becomes clear that the bully dance was neither good nor bad, but a situation that had equal gains and losses. As Mary Ann began to see the benefits of being able to interact with friends, go to movies and just hang out, her whole sense of herself evolved in new ways. She no longer complained about school or being the recipient of teasing and hurtful comments. As well, her "illnesses" have all but evaporated. She is a vibrant teenager, engaged in taking control of her life. She has had this stunning transformation in part because she understands the dance of bullying. Furthermore she can and does apply these laws of conservation and symmetry to other aspects of her life.

> **... the bully dance was neither good nor bad,
> but a situation that had equal gains and losses.**

Example 2—Timothy

Timothy was almost five years old when I first met him. He was bright and articulate. He lived with his mom and dad and a 2-year-old brother. Both parents were very loving to Timothy. Timothy had been ejected from two day care centers for aggressive behaviour before registering at the one I directed.

In our centre, Timothy consistently displayed aggressive behaviour towards the other children. His aggression took the form of hitting, punching, pushing and verbal assault. It became apparent he needed our assistance immediately.

Due to his chronological age, there were three specific factors that needed to be taken into consideration when we intervened with this 5-year-old child.

1.   Much of the intervention work was done by the educator through careful observation and recording of the child's behaviour. Then, as situations presented themselves teachers immediately and meticulously helped the child to see the impact of his behaviour on self and others. *And it was crucial that this be done without blame or chastisement. In other words, a balanced or symmetrical approach was required, i.e., absent of a positive or negative emotional charge.*

2.   Since 5-year-olds have only basic abstract thought processes, *it was difficult for Timothy to integrate past, present and future.* As well, he had difficulty seeing both sides of a situation simultaneously. So, the educator needed to use her own creativity to assist him to understand in ways that made sense to him.

3.   And since *children learn from their own experiences and the modelling of older students or adults,* the educator needed to draw on these resources to assist Timothy in his learning.

Let's take a look at the laws of conversation and symmetry at play as Timothy engaged in the bully dance (See table 1.2).

Table 1.2 Timothy's Gains & Losses		
7 Areas of Life	+ Gains +	- Losses -
Spiritual Inner Voice; Sense of Purpose; Vital Spark	+ Gained some confidence in his ability to listen to his inner voice in spite of others.	- Lost some of his vital spark or enthusiasm for life.
Mental Self-Appreciation, Self-Confidence, Mental Acuity	+ Gained some self-confidence in the face of opposition.	- Lost some self esteem when others rejected him.
Vocational Education, Career, Purposeful Work	+ Gained some knowledge and skills in independent play by building intricate structures.	- Lost some time from purposeful play due to the conflict around him.
Financial Wealth, Managing Resources; Self-Worth	+ Gained self-worth by learning to depend on himself and value his work/play as he showed value for his creations.	- Lost some of the wealth of learning that comes from relationships with peers and adults.
Familial Connectedness, Family Relationships, Harmony	+ Gained some connectedness to his own family who cloistered him to protection him.	- Lost some of the connectedness with his day care family where he felt isolated.
Social Friends, Colleagues Circle of Influence	+Gained influence among some of his peers from his expertise in his play explorations.	- Lost some of the affection and friendships and affection he sought from his day care mates.
Physical Energy, Wellness, Health	+Gained skills in health maintenance by managing the stress of conflict.	- Lost his sense of balance or wellness at the unfairness of the situations in which he saw himself.

Once we recorded Timothy's behaviour, my colleagues and I chose to use puppetry, storytelling and role playing as tools for Timothy in his new learning about himself. We also included other children from his play group. We reconstructed Timothy's bully dance experiences with the other children. Following each activity, a teacher would lead a discussion on what the children saw unfold before their eyes. The teacher would facilitate a caring discussion on the implications for all parties: the bully, the bullied and the observer(s). Then, because we knew about the bully dance and laws of conservation and symmetry, we worked to assist Timothy (and the other children) through the activities to replace the bullying and bullied behaviours with a more equitable behaviour. We modeled these new behaviours for the children and had the children, including Timothy, model it back to us using the same tools—role playing, puppetry or storytelling.

To further assist Timothy to manage his frustration and impulsive behaviours, we helped him learn and practice self-control techniques. This involved identifying where in his body he first noticed he was losing control. Then, instead of hitting or yelling, he learned to figure out what he could do instead, before the bullying behaviour occurred. Together, we came up with a plan that he would remove himself from the situation and go to a quiet place, which we set up in the corner of a room using pillows, a blanket, books and puzzles. Here he would initiate very specific relaxation activities such as resting, reading, breathing exercises, or doing puzzles. When he had regained self-control he then returned to his group.

Timothy was a clever child. He caught on quickly. He could be seen walking through the hall and when asked where he was going he would reply, "I am going to be by myself." There was no lecturing, chastising, just trust that he could learn to handle his own behaviour in a socially-acceptable manner. Just think: don't we as adults walk away from a situation that is potentially volatile, catch our breath, calm our emotions, then return to work it out? Many children learn this by watching and listening to others. However, social skills and emotional regulation are difficult for other children and require caring, knowledgeable adults to assist them by designing learning events.

The same process was utilized for the children who were bullied. They were assisted in helping to replace their behaviours as well. So, instead of crying or giving in to the bullying behaviour of their peers, they learned and practiced such behaviours as using a "brave voice and brave talk" while telling someone to stop. We used the same techniques as used in good coaching. In fact, we called the technique our "coaching method."

The Law of Symmetry and the Observer

A bystander or observer has at least four choices when part of a bullying event:

1. To do nothing
2. To intervene and rescue the bullied
3. To intervene and punish the bully
4. To intervene and initiate a learning situation for all concerned

From our observations during our years of teaching, many educators, with the best of intentions, do two things: they rescue the bullied and punish the bully. And since there has been no opportunity for the emotional charges toward each other to come to balance, the imbalance remains and both parties in the dance move on to new partners or to new events with the same partners. Thus the behaviours continue or even increase, sometimes in the same form, sometimes in a different form. For example, when bullying in the school yard is punished one often sees a rise in neighbourhood bullying or cyber bullying through the Internet. See figure 1.5.

Figure 1.5 - The Dance of Bullying for an Unenlightened Observer

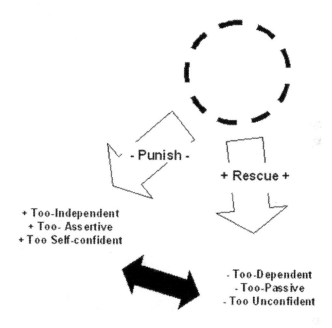

- Punish -

+ Rescue +

+ Too-Independent
+ Too- Assertive
+ Too Self-confident

- Too-Dependent
- Too-Passive
- Too Unconfident

Let's look at this from within the laws of conservation and symmetry and ask ourselves some questions.

1. If I rescue this bullied child am I helping him to learn what to do instead of "giving up on himself" when he encounters bullying again?

2. If I punish this bullying child is she learning what to do instead of this aggressive, bullying behaviour?

The answer to both questions is a resounding "no." For you see, in nature there are no vacuums. If you pull a weed out and don't plant a flower, another weed will soon take its place. It is the same with the human condition; we need to replace an old behaviour with a new one if we are to learn and grow. Otherwise, the behaviours will repeat themselves in new situations until we learn the lesson. When we learn the lesson, we evolve to new places of application and understanding.

> **... we need to replace an old behaviour with a new one if we are to learn and grow.**

As an observer or educator in these situations it is imperative that we understand our role and ensure that we:

1. Remain neutral and balanced
2. Understand clearly that this is a learning opportunity for both individuals and all observers
3. Suspend one-sided judgements, believing that we have the expertise and the wisdom to assist these children
4. Demonstrate, with certainty, how to think about the experience as a learning tool for the growth of each of the participant in the dance
5. Demonstrate, with clarity, a more useful behaviour to the bullied, the bully and the observers
6. Give each person an opportunity to practice the new behaviours in a supportive environment

In this way, all who are involved in such experiences are viewed as learners who need assistance from those who have already learned. Otherwise, we run the risk of creating more and more one-sided perceptions of blaming and victimization, which perpetuates and exacerbates the occurrences of this common phenomenon.

Have we tweaked your interest? Can you see how this approach is different from others you have learned? Is it starting to make sense to you that as a human species we follow the laws of nature like everything else in our universe?

Let's review, and then move on to chapter two, where we will explore how you were bullied.

The Seven Key Chapter Points

1. Bullying is a natural phenomenon that has always been part of the human experience, and always will be, because it serves a useful function in the evolution of the social skill set of the human species.

2. By understanding the scientific laws of conservation and symmetry, educators and educational systems can establish a simple and practical means of dealing with the bullying phenomenon.

3. All parties in any bullying situation could learn to view their experience as an important learning tool that enables them to grow in self-appreciation and to move forward with their lives.

4. Those who have the responsibility to assist a person in working through a bullying experience need to first demonstrate to each party of the bully dance that there are no victims or perpetuators but rather symmetry and a balance to the event.

5. Those who have the responsibility to help others work through a bullying experience need to be able to demonstrate to a person labelled a bully that the experiences can help that person to grow and evolve as a human being.

6. Those who have the responsibility to help others work through a bullying experience need to be able to demonstrate to a person labelled as bullied that the experiences can help that person to grow and evolve as a human being.

7. Those who have the responsibility to help others work through a bullying experience need to be able to demonstrate to a person who has observed bullying that these experiences can help that person to grow and evolve as a human being.

Chapter Two

When Were You Bullied?

The real voyage of discovery consists not in seeking new
landscapes but in having new eyes.

—Marcel Provost

These educators realize that they, like everyone else, have been bullied in the past
by someone. They also suggest it is a very common experience if we look closely
and honestly. What they may not realize yet is that we are usually bullied around
one of our important personal values. And our values are determined by our life
experiences.

Voids and Values

Imagine for a moment you are holding a bag of marbles: half are red and the other
half blue. Each marble represents a significant life experience you have judged
as either a success (blue) or a failure (red). So, this bag of marbles is like your

memory bank of important life experiences. We will tend to believe what we need to believe to make sense of all of these "marble experiences" together.

This collection of beliefs, often called a belief system or value system, will not necessarily be logical, consistent, or even reflect the laws of science and nature. Yet, we will persist in these beliefs for three specific reasons: first, they enable us to make sense of our own personal life history; second, they help us feel safe in the present; and third, they enable us to prepare for the future. As a result, this belief system is fairly stable and takes significant new learning to alter it. We cannot destroy a belief, regardless of what we learn, because this would violate the law of conservation; we can only change its form. However, we can adjust or replace a belief if we have sufficient information to warrant such a transformation.[17]

We take in a lot of information continually through our senses. In order to manage this large volume we engage in three activities that assist us to deal with it. One of the things we do is to *delete or ignore* information that is not important to us at that point in time. Another thing we do is to *distort* information so that it reflects to some degree our current belief system. The final thing we do is to *generalize* information to enable us to use it effectively. We use these three processes to create greater efficiency and the result is a sort of condensed version of our belief system that is often termed our *value system.* We can usually summarize our value system into key values that are found in each of the seven areas of life mentioned above: spiritual, mental, vocational, financial, social, familial, and physical. These core values reflect our critical beliefs and summarize our bag of marbles.

Both our blue and red marbles have a purpose in our life. We often think that only the blue marbles—our successes—are serving us. Conversely, we think our red marbles—our failures—don't really benefit us that much. But if this was the case then it would be another violation of the laws of conservation and symmetry. While we are usually aware of how our successes have helped us create important values, we are often not aware of how our failures have equally served us. Our perceived failures serve us by creating a void that also generates an important value in our belief system.

Specific and important voids in our lives become our most important values, a driving force within us.[18] As educators we have spent much of our lives working with students of various ages, encouraging them to believe in themselves and to appreciate themselves; so, we must also have perceived a void of our own to drive that value in ourselves. Having failed grade seven and spending a lot of time angry and hurting over having to repeat an entire year of schooling, I readily blamed the teacher, not realizing at the time that this same teacher believed in my ability to learn and my need to learn the material in order to progress into my future. This perceived void became a catalyst that eventually drove me to complete a bachelor's degree in three years instead of the traditional four. Without that perceived void of lost time and opportunity, I would probably not have been motivated to work hard later on, saving myself both time and money and creating an opportunity to enter graduate school.

> **While we are usually aware of how our successes have helped us create important values, we are often not aware of how our failures have equally served us.**

A perceived void is a belief that we are missing something or someone in our life. It will be based on one or more significant experiences from our past. Our perceived voids determine our values. Since there are no vacuums in the universe and nothing is ever missing, voids are our own illusions. Dissolving these illusions is part of the journey of learning to be grateful for what is in our life, just as it is. Once we appreciate that the void serves us in important ways helping us to be who we are as a person then we come to honour the void. Then we are in a position to transform the void into any other form that we wish.[19]

> **Once we appreciate that the void serves us in important ways to be who we are as a person then we come to honour the void.**

In psycho-physics, it has been stated by Dr. Demartini that there are more than 4600 human traits identified to date. In other words, there are 4600 distinct behaviours that humans use to meet their needs and achieve their goals. Half of these are perceived as positive and useful and the other half are perceived as negative and useless. *And every single one of these positive and negative traits is used in some form by every person.* That's right, *every person.* In fact, every single one of them *can be labelled as positive and negative,* depending on the perceiver.[20]

Furthermore, while we all have all traits, how we display them differs from person to person. In other words, the traits have different forms in all of us.[21] For example, every one is kind in some form and every one is also cruel in some form. *What differs is only the form of kindness or cruelty and who is doing the judging.* For example, in the same way that there are people who perceive me as kind and generous at times, these same—or other—people may perceive me as rude and impatient at other times. And even though I might not intend to be perceived as rude or impatient, or even kind and generous, the judgement occurs solely in the eyes of the perceiver. So, our intention is not necessarily a factor in how we are perceived. The determining factor is the values held by the perceiver.

> **And every single one of these positive and negative traits is used in some form by every person.**

Let's consider as an example a bullying event in Alice's life.

A student, who was new at my school, was accused of beating up another student. Here is what really happened when a bunch of junior high kids were on their way home from school one day.

I was walking with a group of girls from my class. Just in front of us was a group of older boys, also from my school. Suddenly, they caught up with the new boy, who was walking alone. This boy was not only new in the school but was also a loner.

The group of boys began to taunt him. One boy struck him on the back of his head with a snowball. The new boy kept walking, turning just briefly to see who was taunting him. As the boys from my school got closer, the new boy wheeled around with lightning speed and struck one of his taunters in the face. It was a fierce blow. As blood spattered everywhere, the group scattered.

The group of girls, me included, began to run home, but we were stopped by the older boys. We were warned, or rather threatened, not to tell anyone what had really happened. We could tell who threw the punch to the face, but nothing more. Each girl, to the very last one, swore secrecy. We breathed not a word to any of our parents or anyone else.

Next morning, we were summoned to the principal's office and asked to recount what we had seen. Each of us, without exception, described only the blow the new kid delivered to the boy who hit him but said nothing about the snowball. Within two days the news was all over the school and the new kid was suspended for a week.

Everyone in the school felt sorry for the boy who had been struck by the new kid; everyone, that is, but my friends and me. We felt guilty because we hadn't summoned the courage to stand up to the older boys and tell the truth of what we witnessed. Each of us had been bullied because of fear for our safety and so by association had become part of the dance of bullying.

What specifically were my gains and losses from being bullied in junior high school? Here's how I perceive that being bullied has impacted me and who I am even to this very day.[22] See table 2.1.

Table 2.1 My Gains and Losses		
7 Areas of Life	How Being Bullied Has Benefited Me... + Gains +	How Being Bullied Has Cost Me... - Losses -
Spiritual Inner Voice; Life Purpose; Vital Spark	+ Gained strength in learning to honour my vital spark of being a separate person.	- Lost some confidence by ignoring my inner voice.
Mental Self-Appreciation, Self-Confidence, Mental Acuity	+ Gained increased self-confidence by learning to stand up for what I believe.	- Lost some self appreciation by generating some guilt about myself.
Vocational Education, Career, Work	+ Gained insight into what education was really about, not just math and English.	- Lost focus on my school work for a period of time as my thoughts were on my role in this situation.
Financial Wealth, Managing Resources; Self-Worth	+ Gained in self worth by dealing with this challenging event.	- Lost sight of my wealth of courage and creativity that were available.
Familial Connectedness; Family Relationships, Harmony	+ Gained the opportunity to learn about respect and understanding in my family relationships.	- Lost the feeling of connectedness to my family by trying to keep the event secret.
Social Friends, Colleagues Circle of influence	+ Gained new awareness of the limitation of friendships.	- Lost my trust in systems which don't always protect the innocent.
Physical Energy, Wellness, Health	+ Gained the opportunity to learn how to manage physical energy and emotional stress.	- Lost interest and energy for a period of time for my school life with worrying.

What I noticed as I look back at this event is that there was a pattern in my life that made it difficult to stand up against what others might think of me. Each time I was involved in such situations, I realized that being true to my values was far more important than being true to other people's values. I learned that I live with myself, day in and day out. People and events are transient in my life, while I have to face myself in the mirror every day. Today I appreciate the times I was bullied. I am grateful now because the feelings that came with not standing up for myself helped me learn how to be true to myself and what I value, regardless of the opinions of others.

Now, carefully think back to a time when you were bullied. It could have been today, yesterday, or some time ago. Rest assured: you have been bullied. Think of which of the seven areas of life it occurred: spiritual, mental, vocational, financial, social, familial, physical. What form did the bullying take? Perhaps you were bullied at home, in the community, or in the workplace? Find just one place, one key event and write your story, answering the following questions:

- What specifically occurred?
- Who was involved?
- When did it happen?
- Where did it occur?
- And how were you impacted?
- What did you think about the event and your role in it?
- How did you feel?
- What actions did you take?
- And of course, how has this experience evolved you as a person?

Table 2.2 offers you some guiding questions for your analysis. After reviewing these questions complete the form in table 2.3, by uncovering the information from your own story. What specifically were your gains and losses when you were bullied? Remember, the gains and losses can be in many different forms and will counterbalance each other.[23] Look carefully and you will find them.

Table 2.2 Guide Questions for Your Gains & Losses	
7 Areas of Life	+ Gains + and – Losses –
Spiritual Inner Voice; Life Purpose; Vital Spark	How specifically did it raise or lower your attention to your inner voice, your spirit, your god? How did it clarify or muddle your life purpose? How did it brighten or dampen your vital spark?
Mental Self-Appreciation, Self-Confidence, Mental Acuity	How specifically did it raise or lower your level of self-appreciation? How did it build or destroy your self-confidence? How did it raise or lower your mental acuity?
Vocational Education, Career, Work	How specifically did it challenge or support your educational objective? How did add or take away from your career plan? How did it enhance or detract from your work?
Financial Wealth, Managing Resources; Self-Worth	How specifically did it raise or lower your sense of wealth in any of its forms? How did it impact either positively or negatively how you managed your resources of time, space, energy, money, etc. How did it build or undermine your self-worth?
Familial Connectedness; Family Relationships, Harmony	How specifically did it build or undermine your connections to others? How did it build or undermine your family relationships? How did it create or dispel harmony in your life?
Social Friends, Colleagues Circle of influence	How specifically did it enhance or detract from your relationships with friends? How did it enhance or detract from your relationships with colleagues? How did increase or decrease your circle of influence?
Physical Energy, Wellness , Health	How specifically did it increase or decrease your level of physical energy or stamina? How did it enhance or undermine your overall balance or wellness? How did it build or undermine your health?

Table 2.3 Your Gains and Losses		
7 Areas of Life	How Being Bullied Has Benefited Me... + Gains +	How Being Bullied Has Cost Me... - Losses -
Spiritual Inner Voice; Life Purpose; Vital Spark		
Mental Self-Appreciation, Self-Confidence, Mental Acuity		
Vocational Education, Career, Work		
Financial Wealth, Managing Resources; Self-Worth		
Familial Connectedness; Family Relationships, Harmony		
Social Friends, Colleagues Circle of influence		
Physical Energy, Wellness, Health		

Now as you review the information you have collected from your own past history notice how you can find an equal quantity or quality of costs and benefits that enables you to equilibrate the losses and the gains you perceived to have experienced from the bullied experience. In fact, bullying is neither a positive or negative event, until we place our values on it.[24] For example, the Asian tsunami occurred when the planet Earth "burped," creating what we call a "natural disaster" because we place high values on our lives. We call a tsunami a disaster only because it threatens our existence. Otherwise, it is neither a benign nor malignant occurrence, merely a natural phenomenon. So our perceptions are value-based, not nature-based.

We have emphasized up to now primarily the negative side of being bullied. Now take a moment now to consider the other side, the positive side. How specifically has having been bullied served you today and in your past? Think carefully and jot down one significant way in each of the seven areas of life. You will be really surprised. As an example, I have noted mine in table 2.4. To record yours, use table 2.5.

> **In fact bullying is neither a positive and negative event,
> until we place our values on it.**

Especially notice how each of these significant benefits is tied closely to a significant value in a specific area of your life. So, for example, in the bullying event in junior high school that was cited above, have a look at how it is tied to my values.

Table 2.4 How Being Bullied Has Served My Highest Values	
7 Areas of Life	**How Bullying Has Served Me and my Highest Values!**
Spiritual Inner Voice; Life Purpose; Vital Spark	I place high value on being focused on my life purpose, listening to my inner voice and honouring the vital spark which is me.
Mental Self-Appreciation, Self-Confidence, Mental Acuity	I place high value on increasing my level of self appreciation, enhancing my self-esteem and keeping my mind focused and clear.
Vocational Education, Career, Work	I place high value on life long learning, my educational career and the variety of work that I do.
Financial Wealth, Managing Resources; Self-Worth	I place high value on all my forms of wealth in each area of my life and continually strive to manage my resources of time, space and energy so that it enhances my self worth.
Familial Connectedness; Family Relationships, Harmony	I place high value on my connectedness to the world around me, my family and living in harmony with the laws of nature
Social Friends, Colleagues Circle of influence	I place high value on my special relationships with friends and colleagues and the circle of influence I have built over my life.
Physical Energy, Wellness , Health	I place high value on maintaining my physical energy and balance to ensure I sustain my health.

Table 2.5 How Being Bullied Has Served Your Highest Values	
7 Areas of Life	**How Bullying Has Served Me and My Highest Values!**
Spiritual Inner Voice; Life Purpose; Vital Spark	
Mental Self-Appreciation, Self-Confidence, Mental Acuity	
Vocational Education, Career, Work	
Financial Wealth, Managing Resources; Self-Worth	
Familial Connectedness; Family Relationships, Harmony	
Social Friends, Colleagues Circle of influence	
Physical Energy, Wellness, Health	

Gratitude Arrives in Surprising Ways

By taking the time to analyze our own bully dances using the laws of conservation and symmetry, we can say we are grateful for those times in our life and for those who bullied us. We are wiser, stronger and more certain individuals. Without those bully dances we could not possibly be who we are today.

We have been encouraged to think of the good life as having more pleasure than pain, more positives than negatives, more ups than downs. But in actuality, the truth is, no matter how much we try to say differently, we have an equal balance of both. In every pain there is a pleasure; in every pleasure, a pain. For every negative there is a positive and for every positive a negative. Think of a magnet. If you cut a magnet in two, would that change the negative and positive charge? No, it can't be done. You would just create two magnets, each with a positive and a negative charge.[25] So it is with all of life. So it is with being bullied: it has two sides, a positive one and a negative one. One side benefits, the other costs. Each side is part of a perfect equilibrium.

> **But the truth is, no matter how much we try to say differently, we have an equal balance of both.**

The Seven Key Chapter Points

1. We believe what we need to believe to make sense out of our collected life experiences.

2. Our value system is a condensed form of our belief system.

3. A perceived void in our past drives us to create a perceived value in our future, which creates our present.

4. We display every human trait in some form at some time according to someone.

5. There are an equal number of gains and losses to any event where we perceived we were bullied.

6. Each perceived loss will have a link to a key void and each gain to a key value.

7. Every event in our life, even being bullied, has contributed to key values which we hold today.

Chapter Three

Where Do I Bully?

Our perception is our reality.
—John Demartini

"Perception is everything!"

These two educators are exercising a kind of honesty and courage that many of us avoid. But since we learned in chapter two that bullying is determined by the one who evaluates us, it follows that everyone is probably considered a bully by someone else.

And so where do I bully? This is a tough question because we generally assume that it is a bad thing and causes only pain for others, so we rarely admit to it. Yet we have stated, based on the laws of science, that there are two sides to bullying. What if bullying does have a useful purpose in our own life? And what if being a bully is a universal behaviour used by everyone in some form at different times in order to live their lives and evolve themselves and others?

Most people believe they are being bullied when anyone around them uses what they perceive as some form of authority, to try to control them. There is language that is typically associated with bullying as well. Directives issued to another person—such as you should, you ought to, you have to, and you must—can also be seen as coercive and bullying. What is interesting about the phenomenon of bullying is that it is, like beauty, in the eyes of the beholder. So while we may not perceive ourselves as bullying, others will readily swear to it. Conversely, we may not see ourselves as being bullied where others may see it without difficulty.

Should; ought; have to; and need to are examples of language used to coerce others to live by our values, not their own.[26] Our culture, like any other, has its own set of values that serve to help us fit in and develop a sense of belonging to a family, a group or a community. This certainly has its benefits, since cultivation of a feeling of belonging is a basic human need. The downside, however, is that frequently when adhering to other people's values we neglect our own and thereby fail to honour our own uniqueness. This can bring with it an insidious feeling of being unappreciated and unfulfilled. A long-term pattern of deferring to the values of others can lead to regret, resentment and anger.

> **Most people believe they are being bullied when anyone around them uses what they perceive as some form of authority, to try to control them.**

Perception is also a misunderstood concept. Most people believe that we all share a common perception of what is and is not reality. However, we need only check the literature in experimental psychology and criminal justice to find out that we perceive what reflects our beliefs and values rather than what our senses tell us. Eyewitness accounts of events are often found to be unreliable for this very reason. In fact, as noted in chapter one, most people believe what they need to believe to make sense of all their combined past experiences.

For example, phobic responses to things or events are based on a perception of danger even though, logically, there is little danger, whether it is a spider, a mouse or a public speaking event. Since we aren't born with irrational fears, invariably there will be one or more events from a person's past that will explain where he learned it, either unconsciously or consciously.

> So while we may not perceive ourselves as bullying, others
> will readily swear to it. Conversely we may not see ourselves
> as being bullied where others may see it without difficulty.

The Role of Belief Systems in Bullying

By now you understand that each of us sees our world through our own belief system, which helps us make sense of all our significant life experiences. We see and interpret the world based on our beliefs and values. It is our personal filter for our life's perceptions. When you consider this within the context of the dance of bullying, it helps us understand how children learn bullying behaviours.

For example, if a child grew up with a continual message from his parents or caregivers that he is dependent, unassertive and weak, he might enter school with a *defensive* attitude, that he is powerless and stupid, which can generate feelings of unworthiness and lack of self-confidence. Support and challenge from a teacher could lead him to success in school, which could, in time, alter this belief. He could eventually learn that he is independent, assertive, strong and smart in areas of his life and evolve his belief system to where he has confidence in himself and his ability to learn. Conversely, this child could hold on to the belief he is dependent, unassertive, weak and stupid and become dependent on well-meaning family, friends, teachers and other adults to feel sorry for him and rescue him from life's challenges. He then can become a school yard bullied.

On the other hand, if a child grew up receiving a message of "You are weak and stupid" and adopted a more *offensive* attitude to cope by using self-talk such as "I am not stupid. I'll show you!" this child could turn such thoughts into independent, assertive, self-confidence. This could, build into dramatic actions that manifest as power over others to the same degree as he feels powerless in his own environment in compliance with the law of symmetry. And thus this child can become a school yard bully. The need for power is one of our basic needs and as a species we are driven to meet our needs. And so our choices can be made in socially-acceptable or non-acceptable ways.[27]

It is important to point out here that messages learned in early childhood can become life-scripts because of a young child's inability to hold more than one thought in his mind at a time. You will note we said "can become" and not "will become," for it is always possible at any stage for a person to change a life-script and replace it with one that serves more effectively. Much of the pain of adulthood has it roots in early childhood at a time when a child was incapable cognitively of distinguishing past, present and future connections. As a species we spend our entire life updating our life-scripts in light of our new experiences.

> **You will note we said can become not will become for it is always possible at any stage for a person to change a life-script and replace it with one that serves more effectively.**

Many people think that a belief is like a tattoo, impossible to remove without dramatic psychological intervention. However, beliefs are simply unconscious or conscious choices that we have made in the past about ourselves and the world. Every belief serves the same function: it protects us in some important way. While we cannot destroy a belief, because there are no vacuums in the universe due to the law of conservation, we can and often do replace or update them in light of new information or experiences. Perhaps the most dangerous belief one can have is the belief that beliefs cannot be changed, since it puts a mental limitation on the evolution of a person's thinking.

> **However, beliefs are simply unconscious or conscious choices that we have made in the past about ourselves and the world.**

When you consider the perceptions of a bullying and a bullied person, you can notice right away how they might differ because of unique past experiences. As mentioned in chapter one, research indicates that both partners in the bully dance display very different beliefs and perceptions about themselves and those around them.

Bullying Events in Life

So, if you were to recall times when *you were perceived as a bully*, what form of bullying was it? When did it occur, who perceived you so and why did they adopt that perception? Let us offer some examples Ken collected to get you started.

A Child Bully:

I was the fourth oldest of nine children in my family. When my older brothers were away at school, I was often the "older" brother to my younger siblings. When I was about 10 years of age my younger sister, Mary, who was six at the time, came home upset from playing outside and indicated a "big boy" said he was going to hit her. I learned that the culprit was John, age eight. John's family lived down the street. His parents and mine were friends. I marched over to his back yard where I found him playing. I told him if he ever touched my sister he would be in "big trouble." I can still remember the surprised and scared look on his face when I confronted him. He quickly disappeared into his house. His father came out into the yard and told me to leave his son alone or he would call my parents. I quickly retreated to my own back yard.

I would think that if John still remembered that event he would have viewed me as a bully, as his father did. However, I perceived that I was just protecting my little sister. I have no idea what he perceived Mary had done to warrant a threat to hit her. Nor do I suspect that John's father perceived that his son had done anything.

A Parent Bully:

As a parent of three young children I would on occasion pick up one of my children and deposit them in their room for what I perceived was a serious misbehaviour, until such time as they agreed to find a better behaviour to get what they wanted. From my perspective I was behaving as a responsible parent. But from my child's protests of "That's not fair" or "You're mean," I suspected they believed I was using my physical size and authority to get what I wanted, that I was in fact bullying them.

A Spousal Bully:

As spouses for over 35 years, my partner and I have had the occasional heated discussion about how our children should be raised. I remember on one particular occasion the debate was over the use of the family car. I took a rather casual approach to our children's use of the car. If we had no need of the car then they were welcome to use it. My partner, on the other hand, viewed the use of the car as something that was an earned privilege, only warranted because of chores finished or other contributions to the family completed. I remember my partner saying to me in the middle of a heated debate that I was "bullying her with my modern ideas," while I perceived that I was "enlightening her with my wisdom." Notice we were both attempting to raise our children by our own individual values.

A Professional Bully:

After 25 years of private practice in clinical psychology, I have had several occasions wherein one of my clients/patients has accused me of having an attitude that they perceived as over-bearing, presumptuous, arrogant, bullying, etc. While I may have perceived it as doing my job, being supportive and challenging, or even being a caring counsellor, the other person clearly viewed it otherwise. One vivid example was a mother of a delinquent, drug-using 16-year-old who had just moved back home from his girlfriend's house. As she expressed her frustration with her son, we moved into a discussion of the new house rules he would need to follow to live at home. When I urged her to speak to him immediately about the new rules she had just developed, she got more upset and blurted out, "He will think I am bullying him, the way I feel you are bullying me right now about imposing these rules."

So, everyone at one time or another has been viewed as a bully by someone. It is just a matter of where and when and by whom. So now it is your turn to uncover you own examples by using the following steps.

Step One: Identify Some Examples of Your Forms of Bullying

Review carefully table 3.1. This table identifies some of the various forms of bullying that we have noticed. Then find some of your own examples. Carefully think back to a time when you bullied someone else, as they perceived it. It could have been today, yesterday, or some time ago. Rest assured: you have bullied. Remember the seven forms it could have taken: spiritual, mental, vocational, financial, social, familial or physical. And note the bullying language. Where have you said it?

Table 3.1 How We Bully		
7 Areas of Life	**Our Bullying Forms & Examples...**	**Your Bullying Examples...**
Spiritual Inner voice; Life Purpose; Vital Spark	Imposing my spiritual values on my daughter – "You must consider the bigger picture in life."	
Mental Self-Appreciation, Self-Confidence ;Mental Acuity	Bullying my client on their knowledge, skills and self-confidence – "You must do that".	
Vocational Education, Career, Work	Telling clients what they should do – "You ought to get a more satisfying career".	
Financial Wealth, Managing Resources, Self-Worth	Dictating to my children how they should manage their money – "You should save more starting right away".	
Familial Connectedness; Family Relationships; Harmony	Telling my spouse how she should live her life – "You should make more time for me".	
Social Friends, Colleagues, Circle of Influence	Telling my colleague of my point of view – "You always pick the losers "	
Physical Energy; Wellness, Health	Imposing my health views on a friend – "You never take care of yourself and are heading for a heart attack."	

Step Two: Select a Significant Example

Now select just one example, one key event, and note the details of your story. Write them down.

- What specifically happened?
- Who was involved?
- Where did it happen?
- When did it happen?
- Do you know why it happened?

- What did you think about your role in it?
- How did you feel?
- What actions did you take?

So everyone has been at one time or another viewed as a bully by someone.

Step Three: Study Your Example

Now it is time to uncover how it has served you to have been perceived as bullying someone else. What specifically were *your gains and losses* when you bullied in the story above? To demonstrate we will use the first example we cited earlier. See table 3.2.

A Child Bully:

I was the fourth oldest of nine children in my family. When my older brothers were away at school, I was often the "older" brother to my younger siblings. When I was about 10 years of age my younger sister, Mary, who was six at the time, came home upset from playing outside and indicated a "big boy" said he was going to hit her. I learned that the culprit was John, age eight. John's family lived down the street. His parents and mine were friends. I marched over to his back yard where I found him playing. I told him if he ever touched my sister he would be in "big trouble." I can still remember the surprised and scared look on his face when I confronted him. He quickly disappeared into his house. His father came out into the yard and told me to leave his son alone or he would call my parents. I quickly retreated to my own back yard.

I would think that if John still remembered that event he would have viewed me as a bully as his father did. However, I perceived that I was just protecting my little sister. I have no idea what he perceived Mary had done to warrant a threat to hit her. Nor do I suspect that John's father perceived that his son had done anything.

Table 3.2 My Gains & Losses This Time		
7 Areas of Life	**Gains +**	**Losses -**
Spiritual Inner Voice; Life Purpose; Vital Spark	I learned to honour my inner voice and my sister by protecting her	I learned that honouring my inner voice is risky at times.
Mental Self-Appreciation, Self-Confidence ;Mental Acuity	I learned self confidence in advocating for others	I lost self-confidence when threatened by John's father.
Vocational Education, Career, Work	I learned to respect authority figures.	I learned that my personal power was limited.
Financial Wealth, Managing Resources, Self-Worth	I learned to pick challenges that fit my physical/emotional resources.	I learned not to over estimate my physical/emotional resources.
Familial Connectedness; Family Relationships; Harmony	I learned to appreciate my sister and our family even more.	I realized that I have a limited ability to protect those I love.
Social Friends, Colleagues, Circle of Influence	I learned that friendships can change quickly.	I learned that loyalty can be embarrassing at times.
Physical Energy; Wellness, Health	I learned how to protect myself and the safety of home.	I learned that events can escalate and you are unable to protect yourself.

While we cannot know exactly how this event impacted John, we can speculate as to what ways he may have both lost and gained from this experience. Since we are all experienced at bullying in its many forms, the reader can evaluate whether these speculations have a ring of truth from his or her own personal and professional experiences.

The good news is that bullying is actually an event that we place a value on. And our perceptions are deemed positive or negative based totally on our personal value system. When we view such events from this context, we gain not just a whole new perspective but also an ability to see such events as merely tools that the participants are using to learn to evolve themselves and each other.

There are no longer perpetrators or victims because each person experiences gains and losses equally in the event. Taking this perspective enables the professional to intervene in a more effective manner. What I did was to find the balance or equilibrium of gains and losses that I am aware of due to that experience. I can do it with any event in my past in which I perceived I was bullied or where I perceive I bullied someone else.

> **There are no longer perpetrators or victims because each person experiences gains and losses equally in the event.**

Step Four: Analyze Your Bully Event

Now it is your turn to do a similar analysis on your experience with being a bully, as recorded in Step Two. It is important to be truthful with yourself in this exercise. At first it may seem difficult to find the benefits of what is commonly perceived as only a negative event. But if you persist you will notice that it actually gets easier to find both sides of the experience. *Please note that this step is essential to complete carefully in order to raise you own awareness of the real purpose of the bullying phenomenon.*

Table 3.3 Your Gains & Losses This Time		
7 Areas of Life	+ Gains +	- Losses -
Spiritual Inner Voice; Life Purpose; Vital Spark		
Mental Self-Appreciation, Self-Confidence; Mental Acuity		
Vocational Education, Career, Work		
Financial Wealth, Managing Resources, Self- Worth		
Familial Connectedness; Family Relationships; Harmony		
Social Friends, Colleagues, Circle of Influence		
Physical Energy; Wellness, Health		

As we noted in the previous chapter, for every pain there is a pleasure and in every pleasure there is a pain. So it is with being a bully or a bullied. It has two sides: a positive one and a negative one. One side serves or benefits our evolution as a person while the other has drawbacks that keep us balanced, in perfect equilibrium. You see that each of us has been both the bully and the bullied. In chapter four you will discover the dynamic that draws these people together, and in chapter five just how these experiences can contribute to the evolution of people.

> **... each of us has been both the bully
> and the bullied.**

The Seven Key Chapter Points

1. Whether bullying is occurring is determined by the perceiver.

2. A perceiver judges whether he is being bullied by his own values.

3. We believe what we need to believe about ourselves and the world to make sense of our collection of life experiences.

4. Beliefs are not tattoos but rather unconscious or conscious choices.

5. Our values are determined by our belief system, which is established by our life experiences.

6. There are no perpetuators or victims in bullying because each person gains or loses equally in the event.

7. Bullying is a universal behaviour used by everyone at different times and in different forms.

Chapter Four

The Dance of Bullying

The great truths of nature cannot be arrived at merely by
close observation of the external world.

—Albert Einstein

These two teachers are talking about bullying as a form of communication. How do two people end up relating to each other in this way? In this chapter you will discover just how the bully and the bullied are drawn together in a synchronous dance.

When we think of a dance that is well-executed we think of movement that is perfectly counterbalanced, with each partner responding unconsciously to the movements of the other in time to the underlying music. It is that way in the dance of bullying. Since you explored your own experiences of being bullied and being a bully in the previous two chapters, it is likely clearer to you there is a dance here too. It is the dance of life, the dance of evolution. Let us take a closer look.

In our universe, everything is balanced. Nature seeks a balance in all things. For example in the natural world the earth and other planets are balanced around the sun; water seeks its own balance; summer balances winter; wind is high and low air pressure systems seeking balance; humans are balanced upright with two counterweights of arms, legs, eyes, ears, etc; one can't depress without first having a fantasy, the bigger the fantasy the bigger the depression and so on. If one takes the time to look, one can find evidence of the law of symmetry everywhere around us.

So when we look at the balance in nature, it is clear that there is right *and* wrong and nature operates only in balance. Now take a look again at human thinking, the majority of which is in terms of right *or* wrong. As human beings, we think off balance or out of balance. We exaggerate or minimize what is based on our own perceptions of how we think a situation ought to be according to our values. We *imagine* that something has more gain than loss, more positive than negative, more ups than downs, more pain than pleasure or vice versa. The truth lies in the laws of conservation and symmetry, which when applied to humans Dr. John Demartini called "The Great Discovery". He states that

> in our lives we will not receive nice, positive, praise, honour or support without simultaneously receiving an equal and opposite mean, negative, reprimand, humiliation or challenge. This will occur either from ourselves or others, from one or many people, from males or females, and be noticed in our perceived reality or in our virtual reality—our imagination.[28]

We exaggerate or minimize what is based on our own perceptions of how we think a situation ought to be according to our values.

To assist with clarity, let's explore an example. Think of a time when someone put you down. Write down the name of that person and the situation. Now, at the very moment you were being put down, who was lifting you up? Look carefully. It could be yourself or another, a male or female, one or many people, real or virtual. It must be at the very same moment in time. When you look very carefully, you will find it.

Alice has an example:

One day I was in my office with a student who was upset because I was holding her accountable for her choices. She ranted about how unfair I was as well as putting me down regarding my teaching ability. In my mind, however, I remained calm, cool and collected because my mind went to another student who had recently made it a point to thank me for challenging her to rise to her potential in her work.

Both the put-down and the lifting up came to me at precisely the same moment. Until I understood this law of symmetry, I would often assume the student's responsibility; in other words, buy into her perceptions and values while second guessing myself. I might think that perhaps there was something I could have taught better or perhaps I should have recognized her struggles more quickly. I used to worry a lot about my students, sometimes to the point where I felt they literally ran my life and consumed a lot of space and time in my mind, and I was often stressed. I also felt guilty that I was causing them pain when I was firm in holding them accountable for their actions, whether it was their treatment of others or their lack of responsibility and commitment. This guilt also stressed me since many of the students came from homes that were labelled by society as "disadvantaged socially and financially." And so, at times I thought that society, which included me, was somehow to blame. I was into a lot of blame, I took on a lot of my students' responsibility and, although I loved teaching, I was beginning to stress myself, feel very tired and question whether I ought to continue my career.

If nature does create a balance in all things and everything has two sides, then:

- Rescue is the illusion of one-sidedness
- For every right there is a wrong
- For every attraction a repulsion
- For every elation, a depression
- For every support, a challenge
- For every upper, a downer.

At a systems level we can't manage any behaviour in ourselves or others in which we can't see both sides. In other words, we can't manage any behaviour in which we can't see both the costs and the benefits and their balance.

For example, if we don't create balance in our work life, then we tend to exaggerate or minimize it. If we exaggerate it we create workaholics and if we minimize it we create underachievers. In the same way, if we don't see benefits and costs to our eating style we can create obesity or anorexia nervosa. So with bullying, if we can't see both sides we can't intervene and manage it.

A recent public event demonstrates this in relation to violence. Recall the violence of September 11, 2001; what we now term "9/11." Recall what happened at the very moment the first plane crashed into the twin towers. If you remember, people at the site immediately started helping each other and contacting loved ones. In other words, there was an outpouring of the opposite of violence and hate: support and caring. At that moment of mass violence there was an equal outpouring of mass caring. And it was not only from those at the scene but from individuals and groups around the world. See the balance?

It doesn't matter what happens: one can see the other side, the balance, if one looks for it. "The truth of the natural laws of conservation and symmetry is that we can not rise above a traumatic experience until we can identify and appreciate how it serves us."[31] We certainly can identify the pain associated with 9/11 but have we stopped to look also at the corresponding benefits to us individually and as a society in the seven areas of life?

> **So with bullying,**
> **if we can't see both sides**
> **we can intervene and manage it.**

Let's review a few benefits to draw your attention to the other side of 9/11. Table 4.1 shows a few that have begun to be recorded in the media.

Table 4.1 – The Gains from September 11th, 2001	
7 Areas of Life	✦ Gains ✦
Spiritual Inner Voice; Life Purpose; Vital Spark	Gained an opportunity to increase our focus our own inner voice, our own ethics and increased attention on the similarities of spiritual values.
Mental Self-Appreciation, Self-Confidence; Mental Acuity	Gained an opportunity to appreciate our self, our freedom and our own life.
Vocational Education, Career, Work	Gained an opportunity to affirm our decisions, careers and work and how it contributes to our society.
Financial Wealth, Managing Resources, Self-Worth	Gained numerous business opportunities in security and other related disciplines creating employment and opportunities for many.
Familial Connectedness; Family Relationships; Harmony	Gained an opportunity to appreciate our own connectedness to our family and the harmony we have in our life.
Social Friends, Colleagues, Circle of Influence	Gained an opportunity to appreciate our own friends, colleagues and circles of influence we sometimes take for granted.
Physical Energy; Wellness, Health	Gained improved safety precautions in many forms of travel world wide which frees people's energy and promotes wellness and health.

We are sure you can think of many other ways and many other examples of how 9/11 served our entire planet. When we consider both sides of 9/11 we begin to realize that viewing it from this enlightened perspective enables us to move forward from it with more wisdom and inspiration. The same is true for our life experiences; we can't rise above our traumatic life experiences until we can own them and identify how they serve us.

Take a closer, more personal look. Think of someone you've met who has had what you perceive as a horrendous past but somehow has turned that apparent void into a value that has inspired his life and even inspired others? There are examples everywhere. Check out family ancestors, family members, friends, neighbours, colleagues, public figures, etc. We, like you, have relatives who survived, worked and raised families through the Great Depression, World War I, and World War II, the Korean War, the Vietnam War, the Gulf War and other dramatic and challenging events. To sustain one's commitment to go on in the face of such challenges would require each person to consciously or unconsciously find counterbalancing reasons to move forward and let these experiences go. While each person's would be unique, the task would be similar.

The Bullied

At this point, perhaps you are wondering what this has to do with bullying. Actually, just about everything! To really understand we must look at how voids and values are created. First, let's take the bullied individual, often termed the "victim."

The person who is seen as the victim in the bullying dance is the one who is being rescued from the bully. Rescuing is usually done with the best of intentions. It is to make life easier for the victim and to assist him in some way. What might the victim see as missing in his life that can become a value, so as to drive his behaviour?

Perhaps this is a child who perceives himself as powerless and stupid because he can't see a way to change the situation, who has not been free to make decisions or believes he is not as good or as smart as others. And as a result, he is practiced at getting others to stand up for him, protect him and even think for him.

If you recall your own professional and personal experience, could it be that these might be some of the beliefs held by a victim in your own memories? Could these also be some of the perceived voids that a child needs to experience fully to break through and become more independent, assertive and self-confident?

So exactly what is the dance here? What are the two sides of this "victim coin"? Let's take a look.

Table 4.2 The Balance for the Bullied		
7 Areas of Life	**+ Advantages of Rescuing the Bullied +**	**- Disadvantages of Rescuing the Bullied -**
Spiritual Inner Voice Life Purpose Vital Spark	+ Child may learn to protect his Vital Spark.	- Child may dampen his Vital Spark.
Mental Self-Appreciation Self-Confidence Mental Acuity	+ Child may learn his safety is important to others.	- Child may lose some of his independence and certainty.
Vocational Education Career Work	+ Child may learn self-protection through seeking out authority figures.	- Child may learn to not seek creative solutions to problems within themselves.
Financial Wealth Managing Resources Self-Worth	+ Child may learn he/she is safe from some of the usual childhood risks.	- Child may lose significant self-worth.
Social Friends Colleagues Circles of influence	+ Child may avoid the challenges of those who are more socially interactive.	- Child may adopt a victim mentality of helplessness.
Familial Connectedness Family Relationships Harmony	+ Child may feel more connected having identified common adversary.	- Child may learn fear and embarrassment over their role in the events.
Physical Energy Wellness Health	+ Child may be more assured of their physical safety.	- Child may be less physically and socially active because of fear of experiences outside his/her safe zone.

Of course, this is merely the tip of the iceberg. The trick is to find at least 10 examples of how being bullied is both positive and negative to the very same degree. Then, and only then, will you be able to see that being the victim of bullying actually holds equal amounts of costs and benefits. The truth is that being perceived as a victim and being constantly rescued by well-meaning people further victimizes the child. And the child keeps attracting similar events into her life to help her learn how to see herself as a *victor* over her fear and not a *victim* any longer.

To broaden and deepen your understanding of this side of the bullying dance add at least 10 of your own examples to the table above.

What about the Bully?

What might be a value that drives bullying behaviour? Dr. William Glasser, in his Choice Theory Model of human behaviour, describes four psychological needs that, like the body's physiological needs, are genetically encoded into human beings.[29] The four psychological needs are:

1. Freedom or Choice
2. Power or Recognition
3. Love or Belonging,
4. Fun or Progress

Could it be a need for love/belonging and power/recognition that the child thinks he doesn't have already that motivates? Could this perceived void become a value that drives his behaviour? We believe that the child who carries the label of bully does not feel a sense of belonging and is infatuated with having power over others. This is due to the child's perception that he is powerless in specific areas of his life and does not feel valued in important areas of his life.

It is this façade, or "persona of self-righteousness" (I am right and you are wrong) that will attract a person with the opposite charge, a "self-wrongeous" persona, (I am wrong and you are right) a victim. They are both being driven toward each other unconsciously by two laws of nature, the laws of conservation and symmetry. Furthermore, this child has a high emotional (positive) charge on this type of behaviour, which therefore runs his life. Such a child fails to see where he has power in his life and therefore tries to get it by being powerful over others. He becomes a "careless" communicator when his values become the most important and he fails to recognize the values of others.[30]

Just for a moment, let's recall some of the types of bullying we humans engage in that we've already discussed. Bullying can take form in all seven areas of life (See figure 4.1). So spiritual bullying occurs, as does mental, vocational, financial, familial, social and physical. It can take place between child and adult, adult and child, child and child, and adult and adult.

Figure 4.1 – The Seven Areas of Life

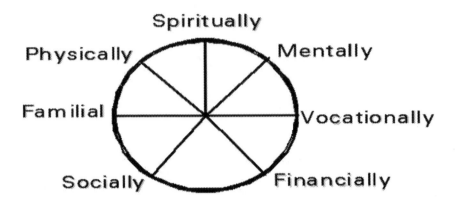

The Seven Areas of Life

Some examples are:

Spiritual: Perceived pressure to take on the beliefs of others, especially as they relate to their own connection to the world and to act contrary to personal values, e.g., religious beliefs and practices

Mental: Perceived coercion to think a certain way about our self or the world in general or to make certain decisions in a certain direction, e.g., self-esteem, sexual orientation or racial beliefs

Vocational: Perceived coercion to pursue a certain career path or area of study that is not our own and denies what is purposeful to us, e.g., academic focus, recreational interests or hobbies

Financial: Perceived coercion to allocate resources in a certain manner. Resources can be tangible or intangible, such as money, time, attention, energy and any other resource we deem valuable to us, e.g., part time work, contributing to family or priority setting

Familial: Perceived coercion by family to follow certain family values, mores or traditions that are no longer shared by the individual, e.g., curfews, house rules or family customs

Social: Perceived pressure to comply with specific rules, values and behaviours in order to belong or fit in with certain groups that we value, e.g., drug use, sexual practices or clothing styles

Health: Perceived pressure as to how we should act and think in relation to our physical and emotional health, our well-being and vitality, e.g., fitness, body image or birth control

For preteens and teens involved in bullying, each area of life can be a source of perceived pressure, especially given the limited amount of previous experience and practice these children have had in some of these areas.

Now Let's Look at the Observer

As the observer or the adult who handles the bullying dance, yours is a most important role. Traditionally, adults will try to rescue the victim and punish the bully. In essence, we try to save the victim from the bully and the bully from himself. And, as has been reported, time and again the bullying continues because we haven't yet understood the laws of conservation and symmetry and how they are operating inside this event. These laws explain why, when we try to save people from valuable learning opportunities, we actually drive them to seek another opportunity unconsciously. In so doing we perpetuate the event rather than resolve it. Let's explore this more fully.

Adults who try to save children from their own need to learn usually fail to use *caring communications*. "Caring communications occurs when one person is able to communicate their own values *inside* the other person's values."[31] In the case of bullying, in order to begin to intervene and connect effectively with each person in the bully dance, we need to first identify the values of each partner.

How does one do this? It takes awareness, it takes effort and it takes demonstrated respect for each child in the form of *neutrality*. It is not difficult. We can achieve this by spending some time talking to each child and listening carefully to what is important to him or her, *without judgement*.

> **Caring communications occurs when one person is**
> **able to communicate their own values**
> *inside* **the other person's values.**

Now a very important point we want you to remember. You know from chapters two and three that you have played both the victim and the bully throughout your own life. You have by now balanced your charge and can see how being a bully and being bullied have equal benefits and drawbacks. Since you have applied this personally you have now positioned yourself in a state of neutrality. You now have no emotional charge on this issue. You see that the laws of conservation and symmetry are at play here and that by seeing one child as a victim and the other as a perpetrator you are actually perpetuating a one-sided way of thinking, an illusion of sorts that contributes to the problem. There can be no other outcome.

So, you may be saying, "I now know what is going on in bullying, but what do I do to assist these children?" Well, we will be dealing with this next, in chapter six. At this point, you will find it useful to know that your role needs to reflect the following to intervene decisively:

1. Recognize there are no victims and there are no perpetrators, just two people needing to learn.

2. Honour the fact that, while children have the same needs as adults, they have unique values that will determine their behaviour.

3. Exercise self-control, using caring communications in all interactions.

4. Communicate your values inside their values so as to be heard.

5. Determine what social skills each child needs to learn and develop a plan, through coaching, to teach them what to do instead of playing out the role of bully or the victim.

6. Support and challenge each child to be successful by offering them specific feedback and suggestions.

7. Continually evaluate and adjust your intervention as required.

With this approach you can then share with others one of the most powerful and inspirational discoveries of your work life. For you will know that no one receives niceness, positivity, praise, honour or support without simultaneously receiving an equal and opposite amount of meanness, negativity, reprimands, humiliation or challenges, either from themselves or someone else, either in reality or virtual reality.

You also will know that emotionally positive-or negative-charged people will attract a counterbalance in order to learn what they need to learn, because you know that emotional charges are conserved and symmetrical with the laws of nature. What a gift to give to yourself and your students.

> ... know that emotionally, positive or negative,
> charged people will attract a counterbalance
> in order to learn ...

The Seven Key Chapter Points

1. The physical laws of conservation and symmetry apply to all human behaviour, including bullying.

2. The natural world in which we live maintains a balance in all its aspects, so only humans judge anything, like bullying, as off balance.

3. Humans can't manage anything for which they haven't found nature's balance.

4. Rescuing the bullied and punishing the bully cannot address the situation of bullying since it denies the two laws of nature that are operating.

5. There are equal costs and benefits to being a bully or being bullied.

6. Our psychological needs for power and belonging are what drive the behaviours of both the bully and the bullied.

7. Bullying can occur in any of the seven areas of life and the observer's role in it is critical to evolving from the experience.

Chapter Five

The Art of Communicating in the Dance of Bullying

As I am so I see.

—Ralph Waldo Emerson

These teachers are asking a question that has mystified many who don't yet understand how the laws of conservation and symmetry are operating in human relationships. In this chapter, you will see how understanding the needs and values of others while honouring our own can provide a vehicle for educators to intervene, so that both the bully and the bullied learn and therefore evolve.

Intention is Crucial for the Educator

As a teacher, you are already aware that communication is critical in the relationships you develop with students. It determines your ability to connect with people, to teach and to learn. You also know that skilled communicators are aware that intention is a critical piece of successful communication and usually quite obvious to the person with whom we are communicating.

One of the basic principles on which many models of effective communication are built is that of intention. Dr. Glasser, in his Choice Theory, as well as many of the most respected psychological theorists, including Carl Rogers, Alfred Adler, Fritz Perls, Milton Erikson, Virginia Satir and others, state in one form or another that each person's behaviour is their best shot at that point in time. In other words, their current behaviour is the most effective one they have, given what they are aware of as options and what they believe will work for them in meeting their needs.[32] This is not to excuse people from responsibility for their action but rather to highlight the old axiom, "If I had known better, I would have done better."

Intention is conveyed through three primary modes, with each presenting a portion of the message. It is often surprising what carries the most information. The actual words we choose represent only seven per cent of the message, while the auditory part represents another 38 per cent. Of course, our body language takes up the remaining 55 per cent. We don't plan to spend much time on an area in which we are confident you are already knowledgeable. We know you know about choosing careful language and that posture and facial expressions are a critical part of the messages we send to our students. But let's take a moment to consider an often neglected area of communication, because we often aren't aware of how important it is and how it relates to our message's intention.

> **... their current behaviour is the most effective one they have, given what they are aware of as options and what they believe will work for them, in meeting their needs.**

What exactly is meant by this auditory part of communication that comprises 38 per cent of the message? It includes the tone, volume and cadence of our speech.[33] The tone we use is our expression of our emotion through our words. The Concise Oxford English Dictionary defines tone as "a modulation of the voice expressing a feeling or mood." Volume is easily understood as the fullness of tone: loud or soft and everything in between. Cadence refers to the rhythm or intonation of speech.

Let's explore this by taking a sentence that you might use regularly in your communications with students and varying its auditory components. See table 5.1 for an example that will assist you. The same statement with the emphasis and/or loudness placed on different word changes its meaning dramatically.

Table 5.1 Variations on Tone, Volume and Cadence		
Sample Statement	Adjust tone, volume and/ or cadence	Message Implied
Class, I need your attention now, please.	**Class,** I need your attention now, please.	A Request
Class, I need your attention now, please.	**Class,** I need your attention **now, please.**	An Expectation
Class, I need your attention now, please.	**Class, I need** your attention **now, please**	A Demand

Now, pick a sentence that you have used in your work with your students. Practice changing the intention by changing the tone, volume and cadence. Explore several different combinations. You will see that, regardless of *what* you say, *how* you say it makes a huge difference in how the message is received because it changes the intent.

Now let's take an example that might occur in a bullying situation. Consider table 5.2. An apparently simple statement like "Why did you do that?" can be said to convey a question in order to collect information or, with emphasis on different parts of the same statement, be perceived as an accusation or even an attack on the person to whom it is addressed. So, even carefully thought-out words sometimes go awry if we are not clear on our own intention.

Table 5.2 Bullying Variations on Tone, Volume and Cadence		
Sample Question	Adjust tone. volume, cadence	Message Implied
Why did you do that?	Why did you do that?	A Question
Why did you do that?	Why did **you** do that?	An Accusation
Why did you do that?	**Why** did **you do that?**	An Attack

Total Behaviour of Communication

We often think of behaviour as just an action by itself. For example, some behaviour displayed by a bully can be very direct such as verbally or physically attacking someone by shouting, hitting, criticizing or ridiculing. Bullying behaviour can also be indirect such as in spreading lies about someone or undermining them in other ways. In a similar way behaviours displayed by a person who is bullied include being verbally or physically attacked, directly or indirectly, so that the child backs away, runs away, avoids or acts regressively in some way. So certainly an action is a part of behaviour. But actually it is only one part.

Human behaviour actually consists of four parts. The doing or action component is the most obvious part. But there is also the thinking component which occurs in our mind, as well as, a feeling component which also occurs in our mind. And the final part is the physiological component which occurs inside our body itself. All four parts are present in all human behaviour.[34]

Figure 5.1 – A Total Behavior

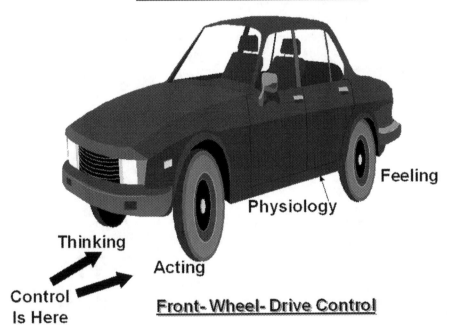

Feeling

Physiology

Thinking

Acting

Control
Is Here

Front- Wheel- Drive Control

An Example:

Think of a car with four wheels and imagine each of the four wheels represents a component of total behaviour. See figure 5.1. Let's let the two front wheels of the car represent the doing and thinking component, with the back wheels representing the feeling and the physiology parts of behaviour. The front wheels (doing and thinking) lead the car and the back wheels (the feeling and physiology) respond to where the front wheels lead them. As it is in the car analogy so it is in life. What we do and think determines and controls our feelings and physiology.

Furthermore we can divide the thinking part, the self-talk, into two sub-components:

1. What the person thinks about *the situation*, and
2. What the person thinks about him *being* in this situation.

Self-talk or disassociation is unique to humans as far as we know. We are the only animal that thinks about thinking, so we can consider how we think about a situation while simultaneously thinking about ourselves being in that situation. For example, consider one of your hobbies, perhaps golfing. You might at one level of thinking be checking the distance, the wind and the club to use while at a deeper level there will be self-talk, such as "I love this game," or "This is great to be able to play with Joe" or "This is good for my health and wellness." See figure 5.2.

> **... we can consider how we think about a situation while simultaneously thinking about ourselves being in that situation.**

Figure 5.2 – Self Talk Within A Total Behavior

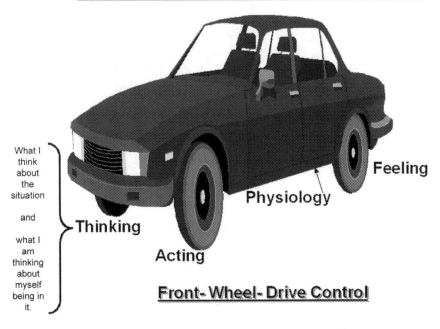

What I think about the situation and what I am thinking about myself being in it.

Thinking

Acting

Physiology

Feeling

Front-Wheel-Drive Control

Understanding the components of total behaviour can assist the educator when working through a bullying event with children. And, of equal importance, it helps the educator understand her own thoughts and feelings as well.

The Role of "Needs" in Communication

As mentioned in the last chapter,

> Choice Theory states that the human brain is like a control system which seeks to regulate its own balance. It states that human beings are motivated to meet five basic needs and that these needs are innate. People choose behaviour unconsciously or consciously, that will help them meet one or more of their perceived psychological or physiological needs.[35]

The human hand is a practical metaphor for remembering these needs. The first four of these needs (the fingers) are the psychological needs of the mind while the fifth need (the thumb) represents the physiological needs of the body.

Looking at figure 5.5, we see that the thumb of our hand could represent our survival needs, the first pointing finger our need for freedom or choice, the index finger our need for power or recognition; our wedding ring finger our need for love or belonging and finally, the baby finger, our need for fun or progress.

As distinct from Maslow's preset need hierarchy of: physical, safety, love & belongness, esteem, self-actualization, need to know & understand, and aesthetic; which he contended is a fixed sequence of psychological development,[36] Choice Theory posits that these needs are hierarchically set by each person based on their beliefs and values. At any given point in time there will be one need that is most important to that individual and *which will drive or motivate their behaviour*. This drive to behave will be manifested as an imbalance, that the organism is driven to restore to balance.[37]

Figure 5.3 – Child's Psychological and Physiological Needs

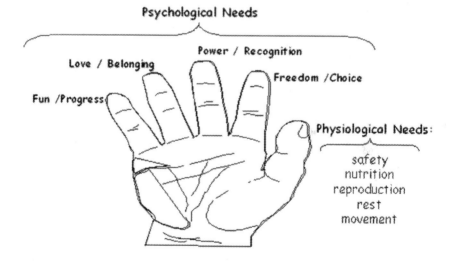

Physiological Body's Survival Needs

Wubbolding in his work, "Reality Therapy For The 21st Century" points out that, "From the standpoint of evolution, survival probably came first. Certainly we can feel the push of this need whenever we are hungry, thirsty, cold or tired. Each of us has a biological need to survive and to reproduce. Many of our human behaviours are related to this need and are automatic to the human organism. The "old brain" keeps these survival systems functioning. There are some functions however where the old brain calls on the new brain to help it out when we need things to help us survive such as acquiring water, food, warmth, movement or sex. It is the new brain or cerebral cortex that houses the psychological needs. This part of our brain has a level of self-awareness and regulates our behaviours."[38]

Freedom/Choice

We live in a reasonably free society and we speak of the virtues of freedom every chance we get. There are at least two primary ways that freedom can be delineated and is often quite obvious in preteens and teens. The first form of freedom is *freedom from the control of others.* The second is *freedom to be our unique self* as we define it. A fundamental manifestation of this freedom is each person's desire for a variety of satisfying relationships in his life. As a social animal, each student needs to perceive that he is not just unique in important ways but also that he is not being controlled by others in important areas of his life.

This is just as true with preteens and teens as it is when we are older. Our need for freedom is met through the choices we make. If we don't have the freedom to make choices and gain some control over our lives, we obviously can't meet that need nor can we meet our other basic needs. As children, we are given choices based on our ability to reason. We start with a choice between "this or that," a choice between wearing the red shirt or the blue one, an apple or a pear for snack, etc. Intrinsic in this of course is the child being held accountable by parents or teachers for the daily decisions he does make. As children learn to make small everyday choices, they grow to be capable of making make more important ones. Thereby, they become capable of making life-altering decisions with confidence as young adults.

Power/Recognition

Among higher animals, humans have by far the greatest need for power. This need is often threatened in larger systems of people like organizations and institutions, where individuals may feel lost or unimportant. Power is seen as a sense of importance. It is not power in a common use of the word (power over someone or something) but rather recognition of one's own innate value. It can be experienced in at least three ways: *self-power* as expressed in such things as physical fitness; *power to manipulate objects,* such as in sports; or *power to influence others* with our behaviours, as manifested in close relationships. And recognition of one's own value is often manifested in respect for self and others. A respect of one's own ideas, wishes and dreams are ways to give ourselves power. And knowledge and learning can build personal power as well.

Love/Belonging

As human beings we have the innate need to give and receive love. Friendship, or a sense of belonging with others, is a vital form of this need. Probably it is derived from survival, as human infants need so much care that love evolved as a strong separate need to make sure that they get this care. We need to have caring friendships and a place of belonging. Children meet this need through their family and friends. It is important to note that both love and friendship need to be reciprocal. It is essential to be able to love and to feel loved by those we deem important.

Fun/Progress

Fun is a basic need because it is the genetic reward for learning. And learning is how we assess our progress as individuals; it is the measure of our evolution. We are born knowing less than all other higher animals, and we have to learn the most in order to satisfy our needs. Evolution has provided fun as an incentive to learn and notice our progress through our life. What is most fun is when we learn something that is obviously need-satisfying. For example, children squeal with laughter when they first walk.

This need is probably one of the most misunderstood in our culture. Many adults believe that fun and enjoyment are something that one earns only when all the work is done. Few understand it is a basic need. Good in her book *In Pursuit of Happiness* notes Mark Twain defines fun as "what you do when you don't have to do anything."[39] Using this definition, it is clear that fun can mean different things to different people. Whatever it is for individuals, it is important to see fun as a basic need and a measuring tool of our growth. Children, up to school age, perceive learning as fun.

Meeting Our Needs

There are individual differences in what will satisfy each of us, yet most people want similar amounts of freedom, power, love, fun and the means to survive. And yet, based on past life experiences, there will be differences in the strengths of the needs between individuals. So for example, if a child perceives that she has been powerless in the past, she tends to work harder to meet that need. In a similar way, if a child does not feel that she belongs, she will then make that her driving priority/need.

> ... if a child perceives she has been powerless in the past,
> she tends to work harder to meet that need.

Our awareness of how to meet our own needs and our commitment to doing just that on a daily basis is vital to our assisting young people in meeting theirs. We cannot give what we don't have. Understanding that as human beings *we all have the same needs*, which must be met on a daily basis if we are to achieve balance is vital. Thus we are reminded continually that each of us will behave in the best way we know how to meet our basic needs. *We must do this because we are genetically wired to do so.*[40]

> ... if a child does not feel that she belongs,
> she will then make that her
> driving priority/need.

The next time a child chooses a behaviour that may be deemed inappropriate, it is crucial to remember, according to most successful models of human behaviour, he is doing the best he knows how to do to meet his needs given his past experiences and level of awareness of his options. *If he is to choose a different behaviour, then it will need to be brought to his awareness and modeled.* Ideally, each classroom teacher will be mindful of this. Ideally, each classroom teacher will strive to reach each child based on his individual needs.

The Role of Values

Crucial to our helping children meet their needs within an educational setting is an understanding of the role of values. You will recall that in chapter two we pointed out that we develop a belief system or value system based on our perceived success and failure in getting our needs met in our past (our personal bag of blue and red marbles).

We behave to meet our needs based on how we want our world to be. We take bits and pieces of our memories, both real and imagined, from our bag of blue and red marbles and hold them in our head as a collection of 'pictures' of how it should be if the world was perfect for us. Choice Theory calls this our 'picture album' in our quality world imagination.[41]

To put this inside a bullying event, we hold in our imagination a fantasy picture album of how we expect people to act toward us. If this picture is one of cooperation, compassion and kindness, and we see a child being bullied by another, it is likely that the initial reaction might be to rescue the bullied child and to chastise the bully. These actions reflect our personal values. However, we know that while this may stop the action for the moment it does not have long-term influence. Understanding how we have come to think about bullying does explain why we do what we do. And it also accentuates the importance of understanding children's needs and the total behaviour concept, so we can communicate more effectively and change what we do to facilitate a different outcome.

Let's explore why a child might bully, what values they are connected to and what feelings would be generated by such behaviours. The "why" of behaviour is invariably based on some need the individual perceives they have at that moment in time. So considering table 5.3, you can see some of the emotions that are experienced by the bully.

Table 5.3 – Needs, Values and Feelings of a Bully		
Bully's Needs	Bully's Values	Feelings Generated by a Bully's Perception of Unmet Needs
Freedom / Choice	To be free to choose his/her own friends	Feel restricted and scrutinized
Power / Recognition	To be important to be listened to and recognized as worthwhile	Feel ignored and unvalued
Love / Belonging	To be loved and belong to a family and or group of friends	Feel unloved and unaccepted
Fun / Progress	To have fun, laugh, learn and grow	Feel discouraged and depressed
Physiological - Safety, Nutrition, Reproduction, Rest	To be strong and safe,	Feel weak and fearful

Now in table 5.4 we can see why a child might be bullied and what values and feelings would accompany these behaviours.

Table 5.4 – Needs, Values and Feelings of a Bullied		
Bullied's Needs	**Bullied's Values**	**Feelings Generated by a Bullied's Perception of Unmet Needs**
Freedom / Choice	To be free to choose his/her own friends	Feel restricted and scrutinized
Power / Recognition	To be important to be listened to and recognized as worthwhile	Feel ignored and unvalued
Love / Belonging	To be loved and belong to a family and or group of friends	Feel unloved and unaccepted
Fun / Progress	To have fun, laugh, learn and grow	Feel discouraged and depressed
Physiological - Safety, Nutrition, Reproduction, Rest	To be strong and safe,	Feel weak and fearful

As you compare the two tables, what do you notice right away? Yes, of course, they are strikingly similar. Each partner in the dance has similar needs, values and feelings during the event.

The Three Types of Communication

Dr. John Demartini, in his work in psycho-physics[42], refers to three types of communication:

1. *Careless* Communication
2. *Careful* Communication
3. *Caring* Communication

Careless Communication

Careless communication happens when we portray our values as being more important than those of the person to whom we are communicating. In other words, "we'll do it my way or not at all." It happens when we believe that we or our values are some how better than the other person's. It happens when we adopt a self-righteous attitude or persona. We kick into this attitude or approach when we want to assert power or control over people or events. A bully's behaviour is an excellent example of careless communication. The bully is assuming his needs and values are more important than those of the bullied.

If the educator also assumes a careless communication style it usually decreases the behaviour for the moment but at the same time increases the bully's resentment and fuels the reoccurrence of bullying in the future. The bully now feels powerless, excluded and bullied as well. And no attempt has been made to understand his behaviour, that is, his beliefs, values, or needs in the situation. *It is important to note that learning to understand the beliefs, values and needs that generate behaviour is not condoning the behaviour.*

Careless communication happens when we portray our values as being more important than those of the person to whom we are communicating.

Let's explore why a child might use careless communication by bullying. What might be a *bully's needs*?

- Bullying can meet the need to belong to a certain group.
- Bullying can meet the need to feel important and powerful.
- Bullying can meet the need to be recognized.

What might be a *bully's beliefs or values* that foster this type of behaviour?

- The bully may value physical strength.
- The bully may value psychological power.
- The bully may value being a part of an influential group.

What are the *consequences to a bully* of not learning other behaviour?

- The bully may continue to use abusive behaviours.
- The bully may continue to build unsuccessful relationships.
- The bully may continue with ongoing imbalancing behaviours.

Careful Communication

Careful communication happens when we make the values and needs of others more important than our own. It means tiptoeing around a person or an issue so as not to make waves. It means giving up your values because you perceive the values of others to be of greater importance. The person who uses this type of communication primarily puts others on a pedestal and berates herself. Adopting an opposite attitude to self-righteousness, this person is said to have a *"self-wrongeous"* attitude. The underlying self-talk may be "You're right and I am wrong." A person who uses this communication style will usually do whatever it takes to please others. Meeting the need for safety or love and belonging is often very important to her. And being bullied is an excellent example of this communication style.

If the educator also assumes a careful communication style it usually decreases the behaviour for the moment while the adult is present, but at the same time increases the bully's self-righteousness and the bullied's resentment, fuelling the reoccurrence of more bullying in the future. The bullied often feels powerless, ignored and bullied even more. And again, no attempt has been made to understand his behaviour, that is, his beliefs, values, or needs in the situation.

> **Careful communication happens when
> we make the values and needs of others
> more important than our own.**

And let's also explore why a child might get bullied? We know that all behaviour has a purpose and consequence. So how does it serve someone to be victimized by bullying?

What might be a *bullied child's needs*?

- Being bullied can offer a sense of belonging, derived from the attention received from adults and other children.

- Being bullied can offer recognition or attention from adults or other children.

- Being bullied can offer safety from adults or other children.

What might a *bullied child's beliefs or values* be to foster this type of behaviour?

- The bullied child may believe that adults will always take care of children.

- The bullied child may believe that one should never hurt another.
- The bullied child may believe that one will always be respected.

What are the *consequences to the bullied child* of not learning other behaviour?
- The bullied child could learn low self-esteem in important areas of life.
- The bullied child could learn helplessness in facing life's challenges.
- The bullied child could learn to be too dependent on others.

Caring Communication

Caring communication is a strategy whereby the communicator cares enough about her own values, as well as those of the other person, *to honour them both*. This is achieved by the educator immersing her own values inside those of the children. This creates a more balanced communication. This is the communication style required of the educator who wishes to resolve a bullying event.

To insert one's own values inside those of another person's requires careful listening. But when one takes the time to listen to what others are communicating it becomes clear what they value most. Having an understanding of the psychological and physiological needs is very helpful in determining what need a person is attempting to meet by his current behaviour.

Understanding the needs and values of the bullied and bully as well as our own enables the educator to act decisively, instead of reacting to situations that occur. In other words, the educator displays self-control, displays a balanced emotional state, and therefore has no need to exert control over the students because the educator is conveying her values inside those of the children.

The educator assists the students to take control of their own behaviour. The educator is the one who teaches and models, the one who shows how to honour one's own values, the one who understands her own needs and simultaneously understands and honours the needs and values of both children in the bully dance. Such an educator is able to communicate her wishes within the context of the child's values to create a learning situation rather than a punishment/rescuing situation.

> **Caring communication is a strategy whereby the communicator cares enough about their own values, as well as, that of the other person *to honour them both*. This is achieved by the educator immersing her own values inside those of the children.**

The Educator's Needs

What are the *needs of an educator* who adopts a careful communication approach?

- The educator may have a need for freedom or choice in terms of what options are available to intervene effectively.
- The educator may have a need for power or recognition in his ability to deal professionally with this challenge.
- The educator may have a need for love or belonging in the form of caring from his students, peers or supervisors in the carrying out of his professional capacities.
- The educator may have a need for fun or progress in the form of a need to learn to deal more decisively with bullying events.
- The educator may have a need for personal safety either for himself or the children present.

The Educator's Beliefs or Values

What might be the *beliefs or values of an educator* who adopts a caring communication approach?

- The educator may believe that she is responsible for creating a free and safe learning environment.
- The educator may believe that she is responsible for continually finding new, more effective ways to deal with the bullying.
- The educator may believe that to maximize learning it is important for all participants to have some degree of mutual respect.
- The educator may believe that every event in the learning environment has value and wish to use bullying in this manner.

The Educator's Consequences

What are the *consequences to an educator* who adopts a caring communication approach?

- They are more likely to create a need-satisfying environment for their students.

- They are more likely to grow in professional skill and competence by being able to approach bullying as a learning opportunity for all concerned.

- They are more likely to generate both respect and appreciation from their students, peers and supervisors.

- They are more likely to create an exciting and advanced educational environment that challenges learners to see all events in their life as contributing in significant ways to their evolution.

Take a moment to think about the bullying events you have encountered in your professional experience. Notice the connections? How do you feel about your ability to assist both the bully and the bullied in choosing other ways to meet their needs and honour their beliefs and values, while meeting your own needs, beliefs and values?

Remember, to change how you feel requires you to change what you do and think. And also remember to adjust both parts of your thinking: what you are thinking about the situation and what you are thinking about yourself being in the situation. Are your needs being met? Are you honouring your own beliefs and values or those imposed by your school or society?

How Caring Communication Serves the Bully

How can caring communication serve the bully?

- The bully is exposed to a teacher modelling self-control, respect, fairness and a willingness to listen without judgement.

- The bully is given support by the teacher and not driven into escalating the bullying behaviour.

- The bully is given the opportunity to explain his needs and values.

- The bully is given the opportunity to hear and learn about the needs and values of the bullied.

- The bully is given the opportunity to learn more respectful and socially acceptable behaviour.

- The bully is given the opportunity to increase self-esteem and self-confidence in meeting his own needs.

- The bully is given the opportunity to take the learning from this event and generalize it to other important areas of life.

How Caring Communication serves the Bullied

How can caring communication serve the bullied?

- The bullied child is given the opportunity to voice his own needs and values.

- The bullied child is given the opportunity to stand up for himself in a safe and supportive environment.

- The bullied child is given the opportunity to learn he has some options in exercising more self-control.

- The bullied child is given the opportunity to develop more self-respect and a belief he has some influence on his world.

- The bullied child is given the opportunity to learn more assertive behaviours

- The bullied child is given the opportunity to develop more self-worth and self-confidence.

- The bullied child is given the opportunity to take the learning from this event and generalize it to other important areas of life.

How Caring Communication serves the Educator

Finally, how can caring communication serve the educator?

- The educator is given the opportunity to enhance her own energy and spirit by knowing she can connect with children in these bullying events.

- The educator is given the opportunity to enhance her own self-esteem and self-worth by advancing her competence.

- The educator is given the opportunity to increase her professional skills in an important area of her work.

- The educator is given the opportunity to increase her own self-worth through sharing her knowledge and skills with colleagues.

- The educator is given the opportunity to expand her circle of friends and peers, who can influence how bullying is dealt with in our educational environments.

- The educator is given the opportunity to take her learning to other areas of her life where it will be useful.

- The educator is given the opportunity to enhance her own well-being and ability to manage the challenges of her professional and personal life.

Adopting caring communication enables all three parties in the bully dance to be respected, learn and evolve.

Let's now consider the use of caring communication in the example of Timothy from chapter one. From observing the educator notes we see that Timothy's values are physical strength, being the leader of the group or activity and being able to manipulate and construct things.

Timothy's needs are:

- Freedom/Choice—to be able to make choices in how he does things
- Power/Recognition—to be listened to by his peers and adults
- Love/Belonging—to feel part of his peer group and approved of by adults
- Fun/Progress—to enjoy his play and learn new ways to create things

The educator's values are ensuring that each child feels he is free, respected, appreciated and learning.

The educator's needs are:

- Freedom/Choice—to enable all the children to have choices
- Power/Recognition—to assist all the children to learn to respect and listen to each other
- Love/Belonging—to encourage all the children to feel part of the group
- Fun/Progress—to assist all the children to enjoy their play and learn new things

The educator communicates her values within the child's, as demonstrated by the following dialogue.

Educator:	Timothy, I understand it is important for you to show your friends you are strong and that you have lots of good play ideas. What other ways can you think of to show them besides hitting them?
Timothy:	I don't know!
Educator:	Then let's work on it together. What are you doing to get the kids to play with you?
Timothy:	I am making them play. I hit them.
Educator:	Did that work? Do they want to play with you?
Timothy:	No!
Educator:	Then let's talk about what you can do instead to get the kids to play with you. When you're with the big kids in your backyard at home, how do you get them to play with you?
Timothy:	I tell them what I am going to do and ask them if they want to help me.
Educator:	Do you think this could work here?
Timothy:	I don't know!
Educator:	Let's practice it and see what happens. And if it doesn't work, we will figure out something else. Okay, let's pretend that I am your friend and you want me to help you build a house. But I am busy over here with my drawing. What could you say to me?

> **Adopting caring communication enables all three parties in the bully dance to be respected, learn and evolve.**

The Seven Key Chapter Points

1. We are all motivated by the same physiological and psychological needs.
2. We behave to meet our needs in unique ways based on our values.
3. We have the physiological needs of safety, nutrition, reproduction and rest, and the psychological needs of freedom/choice, power/recognition, love/belonging and fun/progress.
4. Our values and belief system evolve from our collection of perceived successes and failures in our past.
5. All behaviours have four parts. The doing and thinking parts determine the feeling and physiological parts.
6. There are three ways of communicating: carelessly, carefully and caringly.
7. The bully uses careless communication, the bullied uses careful communication and the educator needs to use caring communication to intervene effectively in bullying events.

Chapter Six

The Demartini Method

We can only change our lives and create a world of our own if we
first understand how such a world is constructed, how it works
and the rules of the game.

—Michael E Gerber

These educators have become aware of a little known fact of bullying, namely
that it is an example of two fundamental laws of physics: the laws of conservation
and symmetry. In this chapter, readers will take a look at the Demartini Method,
a tool that will assist them in intervening in the dance of bullying from a neutral
vantage point.

As you recall, we began by outlining the laws of conservation and symmetry
that are manifested in all of nature. We then went on to describe how people and
their worlds of health, family relationships, social relationships, financial matters,
work, mind and spirit are included in this symmetry. Applying the laws of conservation and symmetry to the phenomenon of bullying, we noted that each of
us has been bullied and has bullied others. Then in chapter two, we asked you to

explore your experiences of having been bullied in your own life. In chapter three, you analyzed your experiences of being perceived as a bully. Then in chapter four, we described the unconscious mutual attraction, the dance, between the bully and the bullied. And most recently, in chapter five, we detailed the art of caring communication and the importance of understanding needs, belief and value systems, both your own and those of the children involved.

Now we are going to look at a simple and practical method to intervene, from your neutral, professional observation point, in bullying situations. While this tool can be used effectively for any person or event that one resents or infatuates, it is especially effective with the bullying phenomenon. It was created by Dr. John Demartini and is termed the Demartini Method.[43]

The Demartini Method and How It Works

The Demartini Method is a specific series of questions that enables both parties in a situation to come to an awareness quickly of how the situation is serving them in their evolution of themselves and their lives. At the same time, it enables them to achieve emotional balance, which frees them to learn from the experience, appreciate themselves more and move on. It is guaranteed to work if followed precisely. The first seven questions deal with the plus side of the perception while the last seven questions deal with the minus side. It is vital to complete all the questions carefully and fully.

Each of the columns in the Demartini Method drives the learner's awareness and broadens his perception of the events. Each column has a specific purpose in assisting the learner to raise his own level of consciousness about the event. Appendix 1—The Administration Guidelines for the Demartini Method, appendix 2—The Purpose of Each Column of the Demartini Method, and appendix 3—The Process of Accelerated Learning of the Demartini Method are found at the back of the book. These appendices offer a more detailed description the tool and its functions.

> **While this tool can be used effectively for any person or event that one resents or adores, it is especially effective with the bullying phenomenon.**

Let's begin by considering the entire Demartini Method tool. It is composed of 14 questions, seven dealing with the perceived positive traits of the perception

(Side A) and seven questions that consider the perceived negative traits (Side B). It can be completed on the person(s) involved or the event as a whole. When followed carefully, the Demartini Method will enable the learner to learn to appreciate and validate the impact of this person on her learning and evolution. Let begin by assuming it is being applied to a specific person rather than a bullying event and that it is being completed by both a bully and a bullied.

> **This method is guaranteed to work
> if followed precisely.**

The seven questions in Side A (table 6.1) focus on the perceived positives traits of the other person. So for example, a bullied person often sees the bully as having traits of fearlessness, coolness or strength, while the bully will perceive the bullied as smart, considerate or polite.

Table 6.1 - Side A of the Demartini Method						
1.	2.	3.	4	5.	6.	7.
What traits do you most like about the person? [At least 10]	What are the initials of those who say you have this trait? [5-50]	How is this trait in the person a drawback to me? [5-50]	How is this trait in me a drawback to others? [5-50]	What are the initials of those who see the opposite trait in this person? [5-50]	Who was doing the exact opposite to the same degree at the same moment to me?	If this person displayed the opposite trait what would be the benefits to me? [5-50]

The seven questions in Side B (table 6.2) focus on the perceived negative traits of the other person. So for example, a bullied person might see the bully as having traits of meanness, cruelty or unfairness, while the bully will often perceive the bullied as weak, unpopular or nerdy.

Table 6.2 - Side B of the Demartini Method						
8.	9.	10.	11.	12.	13.	14.
What traits do you most despise about the person? [At least 10]	What are the initials of those who say you have this trait? [5-50]	How is this trait in the person a benefit to me? [5-50]	How is this trait in me a benefit to others? [5-50]	What are the initials of those who see the opposite trait in this person? [5-50]	Who was doing the exact opposite to the same degree at the same moment to me?	If this person displayed the opposite trait what would be the benefits to me? [5-50]

Examples

With A Bullied Child—Side A

Now let's consider an example from the bullied perspective.

Table 6.3 - With a Bullied Child, Side A of the Demartini Method						
1.	2.	3.	4.	5.	6.	7.
What traits do you most like about the person? [At least 10]	What are the initials of those who say you have this trait? [5-50]	How is this trait in the person a drawback to me? [5-50]	How is this trait in me a drawback to others? [5-50]	What are the initials of those who see the opposite trait in this person? [5-50]	Who was doing the exact opposite to the same degree at the same moment to me?	If this person displayed the opposite trait what would be the benefits to me? [5-50]
Self-confident	Mom, Dad, brother, sister, cousin, math teacher, etc	I feel weak; I create fear in myself; I avoid taking a risk in school; etc.	They could create fear in themselves; They may feel inferior; They may not try as hard; etc.	Our math teachers like Mr. Brown; the older kids in school like Billy, Mary and Sam; Our principal, Mrs. Green; etc.	While he was looking self-confident I noticed that my friend behind me was acting scared of what might happen to me.	If I had noticed the opposite trait of no self-confidence, then I would have learned to stand up for myself and who my real friends were, and that I can be brave when I need to be, etc.
Cool	Little sister, Mom, Dad, friend Sean, neighbour Allan, etc.	I feel left out, I think there is something wrong with me, I feel angry, I am jealous of him, etc.	They may feel left out, they may feel lonely, they may not think I care about them, etc.	Marcy thinks he is dumb, Jeff said he acts silly, the teacher told him to be quiet in science class, etc.	My friend Jill ignoring me when I asked her a question.	If I had noticed the opposite trait of nerdy then I would have learned to trust myself more, and be more assertive, etc.
Strong	My gym teacher, my little sister, Mom, Dad, etc.	I feel weak, I think I am not as good as him at sports, etc	They may feel not as good as me, they may be afraid of me, etc.	All the kids in the grades above us, the gym teacher, his Dad, his Mom, etc.	I was acting weak inside myself.	If I had noticed the opposite trait of weak then I would have felt stronger inside, would have had more self-confidence, etc.
Etc.						

With A Bullied Child—Side B

Now let's consider Side B from the bullied perspective (See table 6.4).

Table 6.4 - With a Bullied Child, Side B of the Demartini Method						
8.	9.	10.	11.	12.	13.	14.
What traits do you most despise about the person? [At least 10]	What are the initials of those who say you have this trait? [5-50]	How is this trait in the person a benefit to me? [5-50]	How is this trait in me a benefit to others? [5-50]	What are the initials of those who see the opposite trait in this person? [5-50]	Who was doing the exact opposite to the same degree at the same moment to me?	If this person displayed the opposite trait what would be the costs to me? [5-50]
mean	Little sister, little brother, my friend Chad, my friend in grade 3 Melissa, my old team mate Cynthia, etc.	I learn how to make friends; I learn who my best friends are; I learn to appreciate kindness, I learn who to trust in the future; etc.	They can learn who to trust in their future; who are their real friends; how to earn lasting friendships; To appreciate their family, etc.	His Mom, His Dad; his brothers Tom and Richard; his sisters Alissa and Allison; his friends Allister and Nick; etc.	While he was acting mean toward me I noticed that my friend Jillian gave me a gentle look and half smile that told me she was on my side.	If he displayed the opposite trait of acting kind then I wouldn't have learned who I can trust and how to show my trust in people; or how good a friend I have in Jillian.
Cruel	Little sister, little brother, Jason, my dog Spike, my Grandmother, my cousin Jill, etc	I learned to be strong, I learned to take care of myself, I learned who my best friends were, etc	They can learn to be strong too, they can learned to take care of themselves and who their friends really are, etc.	His Mom, his dad, his brother and sister, his friend Jacob, etc.	When he was acting cruel I just remembered how gentile and kind my grandmother is to me every time I visit her.	If he displayed the opposite trait of considerateness then I wouldn't have learned to be strong and how to make friends and love my grandmother as much as I do.
Unfair	My friend next door Adam, my old friend Damien where I used to live, my hockey team mates, etc.	I learned who I can trust, I learned how to make other friends, I learned how it feels to be treated unfairly, etc.	They can also learn who to trust and how to make friends and how if feels to be treated this way.	His best friends, Stephen, Drew and Paul,	When he was acting that way I saw Sarah leave to get the teacher to help me	If he displayed the opposite trait of fairness then I might not have learned so much about trust and friendships and how unfairness can hurt people.
Etc.						

Now With A Bullying Child—Side A

Now let's consider Side A from a bully's perspective (table 6.5).

Table 6.5 - With a Bullying Child, Side A of the Demartini Method						
1.	**2.**	**3.**	**4.**	**5.**	**6.**	**7.**
What traits do you most like about the person? [At least 10]	What are the initials of those who say you have this trait? [5-50]	How is this trait in the person a drawback to me? [5-50]	How is this trait in me a drawback to others? [5-50]	What are the initials of those who see the opposite trait in this person? [5-50]	Who was doing the exact opposite to the same degree at the same moment to me?	If this person displayed the opposite trait what would be the benefits to me? [5-50]
Smart	My friend Joey, little brother, little sister, my cousin, my gym teacher, etc	I feel stupid; I feel angry at myself; I avoid asking a question in school; Etc.	They could feel dumb around me; They may feel less than me; They may not try to be my friend; etc.	older brother, older sister, physics teachers like Mr. White; the older kids in school like Jim, Sally and Becky; the gym coach, Mrs. Black; etc.	While he was looking smart I noticed that my friend Paul behind me was acting dumb by clowning around in class.	If he displayed the opposite trait of dumb, then I wouldn't have learned that there are many kinds of smart; or that some important people think I am smart too in special ways; or to believe that I can do better in my school; etc.
Considerate	Mom, my uncle, my friend Joey, my	I feel less than him/her, I feel frustrated that I don't understand how to do this too, I feel left out and backward	They could feel inferior to me, they might think they have to be considerate back to me, They may think I want something from them.	Their Mom or Dad, or brother and sister, or their best friend.	While he was acting considerate toward me my friend Jason was being rude by not listening to what I was trying to say.	If he displayed the opposite trait of rudeness then I wouldn't have
Polite						
Etc.						

With A Bulling Child—Side B

And now, let's look at Side B from the bully perspective (table 6.6).

Table 6.6 - With a Bullying Child, Side B of the Demartini Method						
8.	9.	10.	11.	12.	13.	14.
What traits do you most despise about the person? [At least 10]	What are the initials of those who say you have this trait? [5-50]	How is this trait in the person a benefit to me? [5-50]	How is this trait in me a benefit to others? [5-50]	What are the initials of those who see the opposite trait in this person? [5-50]	Who was doing the exact opposite to the same degree at the same moment to me?	If this person displayed the opposite trait what would be the costs to me? [5-50]
Weak	My older sister; my older brother; my enemy Harold; my basketball coach in grade 4 Mr. Blue; my old team mate Bryon; etc.	I can feel more self-confident about me; I can learn to value more my athletic abilities like playing basketball or hockey, I can learn to appreciate my strength in biology; etc.	They can learn to appreciate themselves in new ways like being aware of how important it is to be a strong person; appreciate the strength they have acquired through the sports they have played, appreciate the strong friendships they have; appreciate their strong	His Mom; his Dad; his brothers Ray and Glen; his sisters Rosie and Jackie; his friends Rosie and Dave; etc.	While he was acting weak toward me I noticed that the teacher gave me a strong, clear scowl that told me I should back off teasing him.	If he displayed the opposite trait of acting strong then I wouldn't have learned that I have this trait to, I wouldn't have learned to be as self-confident, I wouldn't have learned to appreciate my athletic abilities; etc
Unpopular	My brother, my sister when she is mad at me, my former friend Jenny, my neighbour Margaret, etc.	I have more time for my hobbies, I can spend time with my Mom or Dad, I get to learn to be independent, etc.	They can then have time for the stuff they want to do, they can learn to depend on themselves more, etc.	His Mom, dad, brother, sister, close friend Nicole, his cousin Benny, etc	While he was treating me as unpopular I noticed that Melanie, who was standing behind him, winked at me and smiled because she is my friend.	If he displayed the opposite trait of popular then I might not have the time I want for my hobbies and I might not be as close to my parents as I am.
Nerdy	My brother, my little sister, my neighbour Stan, etc.	I have time to really get to know a lot about things like computers, I get to know who my real friends are, I get to learn that no one really knows me, etc.	They can have the time they need to do the things they want, they get to learn who their best friends are, etc.	His Mom and dad, his sister and brother, his friend Nicole and his cousin Julia, etc.	While he was treating me as nerdy, my best friend Joel was asking me to come show him something on the computer because he thinks I am cool about computers.	If he displayed the opposite trait of cool then I might not know as much as I do about computers, or have the good friends I do, etc.
Etc.						

As the learner proceeds through each of at least 10 traits on both Sides A and B, her level of awareness grows by leaps and bounds as she begins understanding that this other person is just like her, with the same traits in different forms; that each positive trait has a cost to her and others who see her with it; that each negative trait has a benefit to her and others; that other people see exactly the opposite traits in this person; that whenever she was challenged, she was supported in equal measure and whenever she was supported, she was challenged in equal measure; and that if she had perceived the opposite trait in this person, it would have had a similar result.

Feel free to utilize the appendices as resources to ensure the learner has achieved the depth of self-analysis to generate new levels of self-awareness and self-appreciation.

With this higher level of awareness of the symmetry in the learner's life experiences comes a balancing of the emotions about the person and an appreciation for the person and the experience itself. The learner realizes that this person was simply a tool that she used to develop herself and her own level of self-appreciation. Because she has freed herself from a limited, one-sided perspective on the person or the event, she is then in a position to move on to focus her time and energy on her other life priorities.

> **The learner realizes that this person was simply a tool that she used to develop herself and her own level of self-appreciation.**

The Seven Key Chapter Points

1. We can find the laws of conservation and symmetry in any event in our life.

2. The Demartini Method enables a person to uncover the symmetry in a bullying event.

3. The Demartini Method requires persistence and dedication to achieve the learning that is possible.

4. Every trait that we admire in others we also have equally, and it has a cost.

5. Every trait that we despise in others we also have equally, and it has a benefit.

6. The behavioural traits of others are merely tools that we use to raise our level of self-appreciation, bullying included.

7. Using the Demartini Method on bullying events frees the learner to move forward in his life.

Chapter Seven

Shall We Dance?

If we treat an individual as if he were what he ought to be;
he will become what he ought to be and could be.
—Johann Wolfgang von Goethe

These educators capture the dilemma of their role as teachers. It comes from wanting to assist their students in learning from bullying but not really feeling they have a strategy that is effective.

The research echoes this view. Dake et al. found that less than one-third of the teachers in their group set aside classroom time to discuss bullying or involved students in creating classroom rules against bullying. They noted that

> teachers perceive post-bullying activities as the most effective means of reducing bullying problems, followed by improved student supervision and by environmental bullying prevention activities ... The findings suggest that pre-professional and continuing education is needed to

improve teacher knowledge about effective classroom based bullying prevention activities.[44]

In this chapter we will summarize why bullying is a tool to help us to appreciate all that we are and can be, and that we are all continuously learning, with bullying being simply a tool for this purpose.

Your Learning

Our intention throughout this book is to present a clear and concise way to look at the phenomenon of bullying. We trust you now see bullying as a tool we use to learn to evolve and to appreciate ourselves and others. You now realize that bullying is a misunderstood phenomenon that has been around since the beginning of time and will, despite our best efforts, remain as an important evolutionary tool until the end of time. What will change will be its form.

Historically, we have seen that as the bullying of one country by another has waned, other forms of bullying such as child and spousal abuse have escalated. As teachers curb bullying in schools we see a rise in cyber bullying. One of the laws of nature we have been discussing, the law of conservation, teaches that nothing is ever missing; it only changes its form. So, we can never eliminate bullying, but we can recognize the new forms that arise and see them as new challenges, new learning opportunities and therefore new growth in our unending evolution.

We trust you appreciate that bullying is indeed an application of the laws of nature and as you acknowledge and understand this, you, as an educator, can assist children to learn to recognize the dance of bullying and to develop new skills and behaviours they can draw on through a lifetime, regardless of whether they play the role of bully, the bullied or the observer.

> ... we can never eliminate bullying but we can recognize the new forms that arise and see them as new challenges, new learning opportunities and therefore new growth in our unending evolution.

A New Paradigm in Bullying

Let's take an observer position, as you bring this phenomenon to a place of equilibrium. This is a place of *presence, certainty* and *appreciation*. As a place of *presence*, it is a neutral place where you can assist the bully and the bullied to see both sides of the dance's equation of costs and benefits. As a place of *certainty*, it is a place from where you can see without a doubt that this event is intended to serve the children's future. And as a place of *appreciation*, it is a place where you feel a sense of gratitude for this tool called bullying, because it serves all concerned.

Couched in the context of Choice Theory, ultimately it becomes a place where the bully, the bullied and the observer can develop new ways of doing and thinking that will impact on how they feel about themselves and others, as well as their overall well-being.

An Emotional Observer

What if there is not a neutral adult but an additional fearful or indifferent observer or crowd who witness a bullying event? For example, it is not uncommon in school yard bullying for one child to assault another while other children watch. Why would these children choose to let this happen? It seems difficult for us to understand. Let's apply what we have learned so far.

If an observer is fearful, perceiving the bullying situation as self-threatening, then he is being bullied also by association. On the other hand, if the observer identifies with the bully in some way and chooses to not intervene then he also becomes an accomplice of the bully. The choice to intervene or not is a real choice based on the values of the observer.

The observer's choice of action will depend on his values. It was noted earlier that because of our past experiences, the pictures in our heads of how we want our world to be, we have a unique set of values that determine our behaviours. We are compelled unconsciously for the most part to live within these values. The determining factor in whether someone will intervene in a bullying event is the question of how high on his value list does this person place such values as fairness, violence, power, rescuing, loyalty and personal safety. "The hierarchy of a person's values will determine their choice of action every time. Each of us will do our best to live by our own values at all times."[45]

An Emotional Observer's Values

As you teach this process to your students it is necessary to help the observer tune into their own feelings and self-talk. Let's use the school yard bullying situation cited in the previous paragraph.

When interviewed by an adult about a school yard bullying event, a child who observed the incident will often speak of the fear of the violence being turned on her. Fear of getting hurt, or even embarrassed, often immobilize other children from intervening alone or even as a group. So, if personal safety is high on a child's value list it can be a huge factor in determining her actions.

Other factors that could be at play in such situations might be that the bullied may somehow be getting what he justly deserves, or the observer may be connected in some way to the bully and through a sense of fair play, loyalty and/or fear may choose to not get involved. Remember, you learned that the one thing—the only thing you can trust about a person is that he will do his best to live by his own values. So, if a child places a high value on his safety, he will do what he perceives he must to live by that value and will avoid situations that will put his safety in jeopardy.

If a child is a friend of the bully and values loyalty above justice, fairness or non-violence, then it is highly predictable she would stand by in such an attack and not assist the bullied. If a child sees the bullied as somehow "asking for it" and values fairness—"an eye for an eye"—then it again is highly predictable the observer would remain in that role, or may even encourage the assault on the bullied, so the bullied gets what he "deserves."

So you can see how recognition of how the bully, the bullied and the observer serve as tools to assist all individuals evolve is crucial to the bully dance. As educators who have a heightened awareness of what is at play here, it is our responsibility to assist the other players to understand it as an opportunity for growth.

> **... recognition of how the bully, the bullied and the observer serve as tools to assist all individuals evolve is crucial to the bully dance.**

The Dance Steps

Will you dance with us by first recalling, then stepping into the rhythm of the dance?

Step 1: We understand bullying is an application of the laws of symmetry and conservation and these laws govern nature and everything in it, including humans and their relationships.

Humans think in terms of right *or* wrong. Nature thinks in terms of right *and* wrong. Nature knows that everything serves in some way to encourage our evolution as a species and as a universe. See figure 7.1.

<u>Figure 7.1 Nature's Law of Symmetry</u>

<u>Nature operates in a perfect balance!</u>

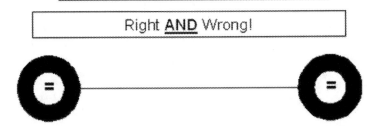

<u>Humans operate in imbalance!</u>

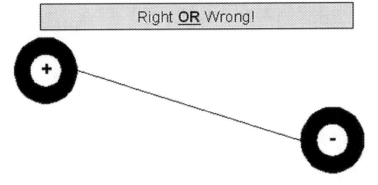

Step 2: We understand everyone has all traits, and since you can neither lose nor gain traits, we know we have experienced being the bully, the bullied and the observer.

Each of us displays in some form all of the 4600 human traits, half of which are perceived as positive while the rest are considered negative. Revisit your own bullying experiences in all three roles: the bully, the bullied and the observer. In light of what you now know, identify how each of the roles served you in each of the seven areas of your life.

Step 3: "We know that as sure as we are born, we will die, and in between, we will evolve. We cannot not evolve. We can choose to learn and flow with the laws of life or we can choose to resist and accelerate our recycling."[47]

If we try to resist our evolution we will be attracted to a similar situation again and again until we learn. When we get that lesson we move on, to be tested in different forms and with different lessons.

Therefore, if we resist the lessons of the bully, the bullied or the observer we stay stuck and the pattern repeats itself in some form, over and over again, just like a dancer with "two left feet" who stumbles and trips over them until he gets the rhythm and is able to balance with both feet and moves in synchronicity to the music of the dance. So too bullying is an exercise in tripping over our perceptions of life, perceptions that won't go away until we uncover the learning that is important to our well-being and evolution and can, without hesitation, participate in the beautiful rhythm of the dance of life.

Step 4: We choose to communicate our values through our behaviours.

Whatever attitude or persona you take on with your behaviours, you will attract the opposite attitude to assist your evolution. The key is to assume no persona, establishing instead an attitude of balance and equilibrium through which you can communicate your values within those of others.

Step 5: We use the Demartini Method to create personal balance around the whole concept of bullying and its traditional perspectives.

Equilibrating, through the use of the Demartini Method, changes your perception of the bullying experience, helping you to create inner balance and thereby opening you to approach the situation from a place of presence, certainty and appreciation—a place of balanced emotion.

Step 6: We understand the impact of caring communications and people's ability to learn from every life experience.

Caring communication assists us in balancing our emotions and helps us develop a deeper understanding and acceptance of ourselves and others. We learn to honour our past, all of it, knowing we could not be who we are without each of our past experiences. We also learn to dance with the rhythm of life, recognizing the pain and pleasure in each experience and that we are exactly where we are supposed to be. This awareness brings an attitude of gratitude for all that is, as it is. In this state, we are open to the many possibilities that lie before us. In this state, as educators of children, we can see clearly the possibilities for growth of each participant in the dance of bullying.

> **... learn to dance with the rhythm of life recognizing the pain and pleasure in each experience and that we are exactly where we are supposed to be.**

Step 7: We know that bullying is a tool to assist our evolution as individuals and as a species.

Bullying has been a part of our behaviour as a species since the beginning of time. We will never eradicate it, but as we understand the dance we can assist others in developing the skills and attitudes to evolve themselves to new forms and new dances.

Rhythm of the Dance

In closing, think of music and dancing itself. The rhythm is created not by the notes or the steps but in the many slight and intricate pauses that make up the rhythm. When you get the rhythm of the dance, the music is truly beautiful.

We invite you to join with us in the dance of bullying by booking a three-hour training seminar, and with the accompanying workbook, learning to assist your students in engaging in the rhythms of their life.

The Seven Key Chapter Points

1. Bullying is a tool or behaviour that humans use to satisfy their genetically encoded needs.

2. An enlightened educator will project presence, certainty and appreciation when intervening.

3. The hierarchy of the observer's values will determine his style of intervention.

4. The bullied, the bully and the observer are all equally served by the event.

5. Nature treats events as right *and* wrong or *neither* right *nor* wrong, while we humans treat events as right *or* wrong.

6. Each person displays some form of each of the 4600 human traits, according to someone at some time in her past.

7. If we refuse to learn the lessons that bullying events have to offer, we will unconsciously be drawn to other similar events until we learn the lesson of self-appreciation.

Chapter Eight

For Parents

Making a decision to have a child; it's momentous.
It is to decide forever to have your heart go walking around
outside your own body.

—Elizabeth Stone

These two teachers share wisdom in knowing the parents have a crucial role in dealing effectively with a bully event. Without their support and involvement, the child's learning may not be maximized.

While this book is aimed primarily at teachers and educational administrators, parents have an essential role to play in bullying interventions. As a parent, it is often a struggle when we learn that our child has been involved in a bully situation. Regardless of which label has been placed on our child—bully, bullied or observer—it often leaves us feeling frustrated and helpless. However, when we realize that it is simply another common learning experience for you and your child to work through, it can free us to intervene in a more effective manner.

Since parents are part of the team that will determine how the situation is resolved, it falls on us as parents to also rethink our own life experiences so we can use them to assist our children in their development. When we take the time to reassess our own experiences and discover how these events have impacted us, it lifts us from the polarizing emotions and worry, which can impede the resolution of the situation.

So, parents are strongly encouraged to do the activities in this book as well. And we also recommend that you encourage your local parenting group or home and school association to organize or host "The Dance of Bullying" seminar in your school.

With the ideas, tools and actions mentioned previously as a foundation, the following guidelines are suggested for parents to consider as you determine your role in resolving a bullying event:

1. Remember bullying is *a learning opportunity* for everyone.

2. *Work closely* with your child's school to ensure a united and cohesive approach to resolving the situation, including seeking out the expertise of your child's teacher or other community resource people who can assist you in helping your child develop new skills to handle this challenge.

3. *Avoid labelling* either person, since it usually impedes learning and resolving the situation.

4. Identify your personal experiences with being bullied and collect the ways they have *benefited* you in becoming who you are today. Check out all seven areas of your life in detail.

5. Identify your personal experiences with being a bully and collect the ways they have cost *you* in becoming who you are today. Check out all seven areas of your life in detail.

6. *Share with your child* how the impacts of being both bullied and a bully have contributed to your own development.

7. *Encourage your child to share her thoughts and feelings* about the situation so you can honour her perceptions of the events.

8. Assist your child in *identifying the other side* to his perception of the events so he can initiate his own learning process.

9. Assist your child in *keeping an even tally* of both sides of her perceptions, so that she can learn and maintain a balanced perspective on these events.

10. Remind your child of *your belief in their ability to learn and evolve* from this experience, in the same way that you have learned and evolved.

Afterword

We can only change our lives and create a world of our own if we
first understand how such a world is constructed, how it works
and the rules of the game.
—Michael E .Gerber

If you have read this far in *The Dance of Bullying ... A Breakthrough Tool for
Teachers and Parents* you owe yourself a pat on the back, because you have displayed the courage and commitment to learn in ways that others do not and will
not. You have taken a risk to explore how the laws of nature apply to one human
behaviour, bullying. Now, of course, your interest is peaked and you are challenged
to take the same law and apply it to other behaviours, people and events that you
have perceived as one-sided. If you continue this journey, because ultimately it is
everyone's life-long journey, you will continue to discover how perfectly balanced
every aspect of our world is and our awareness can be.

We encourage you to take *The Dance of Bullying ... A Breakthrough Tool for
Teachers and Parents* to your school and share it with your colleagues, administrators and especially your students. We have carefully designed it to appeal to all the
stake holders in our educational environments so that we can all put bullying in
a balanced perspective and not miss the opportunities it provides to enable us to
evolve ourselves and each other.

As well, feel free to contact either of us directly for follow up suggestions, questions, or queries. Our email addresses are:

ken@clarendonconsulting.com
a.taylor@pei.sympatico.ca

And be sure to check out our website: www.thedanceofbullying.com. Here you
will find more information on our company, *a designed destiny inc.*, as well as
"The Dance of Bullying" and other seminars we offer.

"The Dance of Bullying" seminar is a fast-paced, fun-filled, three-hour intro-
duction to the ideas and techniques that have been outlined here. We would love
the opportunity to present it to your school or community.

We wish you well in your evolutions!

Conclusion

The Dance of Bullying ... A Breakthrough Tool for Teachers and Parents, has likely brought into question lifelong beliefs and practices. You will decide how and when to use it. Our suggestion to you is to read it a second time and do the exercises throughout the chapters to assist your understanding and bring your own experiences with being the bully, the bullied and the observer into balance. Then, you may wish to you take a look at the exercises for your students or your child and begin the work to help them evolve from "victim/perpetrator" thinking to a place where they can also see the balance of the gains and losses in each role played out in the dance.

As you go through your second read, let us summarize the main points of the book. Listed below are the 21 points that encapsulate this groundbreaking approach.

1. Bullying is a natural phenomenon that has always been and always will be, because it serves a useful function in the evolution of the social skill set of the human species. This is perhaps the most fundamental statement in the whole book. It is the foundation for a paradigm shift in thinking about bullying experiences.

2. By understanding the scientific laws of conservation and symmetry, educators and parents can establish a simple and practical means of dealing with the bullying phenomenon.

3. Those who have the responsibility to assist a person to work through a bullying experience need to first demonstrate to themselves and then to each party of the bully dance that there are no victims or perpetrators, no winners or losers, but rather there is a symmetry and a balance (an equal number of gains and losses) to the event.

4. The perceiver, through his own value system, determines whether bullying is occurring and also judges whether they are being bullied.

5. We believe what we need to believe about ourselves and the world to make sense of our unique collection of life experiences.

6. Beliefs are unconscious or conscious choices and therefore can be replaced when they no longer serve us.

7. Values are determined by our belief system, which is established by our life experiences.

8. A perceived void in our past drives us to create a perceived value in our future, which creates our present.

9. Our perceived voids from the past become our highest values, our driving force.

10. We display every human trait in some form at some time, according to someone's perception.

11. Every event in our lives, even being bullied, has contributed to key values we hold today.

12. The physical laws of conservation and symmetry apply to all human behaviour, including bullying.

13. The natural world in which we live maintains a balance in all its aspects, so only humans judge anything, like bullying, as off balance.

14. Rescuing the bullied and punishing the bully cannot address the situation of bullying since it denies the two laws of nature that are operating.

15. Our psychological needs for power or recognition and love or belonging are usually the needs that drive the behaviours of the bully and the bullied.

16. We are all motivated by the same physiological and psychological needs.

17. We behave to meet our needs in unique ways based on our values.

18. All behaviours have four parts: the doing and thinking parts determine the feeling and physiological parts.

19. There are three ways of communicating: carelessly, carefully and caringly. Our goal is to be caring communicators.

20. The Demartini Method enables a person to uncover the symmetry in a bullying event and to move forward in her life.

21. If we refuse to learn the lessons that bullying events have to offer we will unconsciously be drawn to other similar events until we learn the lesson of self-appreciation.

Well, there you have it. The rest is up to you. We guarantee if the ideas in this book are applied to the dance of bullying, you will experience a sense of fulfillment in knowing you have helped all partners in the dance to see its symmetry and to grow so they can take on their next challenge where they can apply the same laws to other aspects of their lives. This is life's journey for each of us.

Endnotes

1. Richard P. Feynman, *Six Easy Pieces* (New York: Basic Books, 1995), 4.

2. Dan Olweus, *Aggression In the Schools: Bullies and Whipping Boys* (Washington: Hemisphere Publishing, 1978), 4.

3. Roxie Alcaraz. *Fact Sheet—Bullying in Schools,* Riverside, CA: Centre of Excellence on Youth Violence Prevention, University of California, Fall, 2004, 1.

4. A. D. Pellegrini and J. D. Long, "A Longitudinal Study of Bullying, Dominance and Victimization During Transition from Primary Through Secondary School," *British Journal of Developmental Psychology* 20: 2 (June 2002), 258–280.

5. S. Bauman and C. Hurley, "Teachers' Attitudes and Beliefs about Bullying: Two Exploratory Studies," *Journal of School Violence* 4:3 (Oct 2005): 49–61.

6. W. M. Craig, R. D. Peters and R. Konarski, *Bullying and Victimization Among Canadian School Children,* Human Resource Development Canada Applied Research Branch Strategic Policy, n.d., 1–33.

7. Johnson, *SVRC Briefing Paper: Bullying,* University of Arkansas Criminal Justice Institute National Centre for Rural Law Enforcement, 2001, 1–15.

8. Craig, Peters and Konarski, *Bullying and Victimization Among Canadian School Children*, 23.

9. Ibid, 23.

10. Ibid., 10

11. Feynman, *Six Easy Pieces,* 20.

12. Ibid., 59

13. Brian Green, *The Elegant Universe: Superstrings, Hidden Dimensions, and the Quest for the Ultimate Theory* (Toronto: Random House, 1999*),* 169.

14. Leon Lederman and Dick Trebesi, *The God Particle: If the Universe is the Answer, What's the Question?* (New York: Dell Publishing, 1993) 13.

15. John Demartini, *Demartini Seminars: The Breakthrough Experience (Seminar Manual)*. Demartini Human Research and Education Foundation, Houston, Texas, 1988–2007, 10-16.

16. John Demartini, *The Breakthrough Experience* (Carlsbad, Ca: Hayhouse, 2003), 17.

17. John Demartini, *Demartini Seminars: The Demartini Method (Quantum Collapse Process) Certification Training Program*, Demartini Human Research and Education Foundation, Texas, 1989–2007, 24.

18. Demartini, *Demartini Seminars: The Breakthrough Experience (Seminar Manual)*, 36-45.

19. Ibid, 25.

20. Demartini, *Demartini Seminars: The Demartini Method (Quantum Collapse Process) Certification Training Program*, 25-26.

21. John Demartini, *The Heart of Love: How to go Beyond Fantasy to Find True Relationship Fulfilment* (Carlsbad, CA: Hayhouse, 2006), 230.

22. Ibid, 119.

23. John Demartini, *Count Your Blessings: The Healing Power of Gratitude and Love* (Carlsbad, CA: Hayhouse, 2006), 3.

24. John Demartini, *Demartini Seminars: The Breakthrough Experience (Seminar Manual)*, 37.

25. Ibid, 16.

26. Ibid, 16–17.

27. Ibid, 19–21.

28. Demartini, *Demartini Seminars: The Breakthrough Experience (Seminar Manual)*, 36.

29. William Glasser, *The Quality School (New York: Harper Collins, 1992)*, 58-60.

30. Demartini, *Demartini Seminars: The Breakthrough Experience (Seminar Manual)*, 10-16.

31. Demartini, *Count Your Blessings*, 34.

32. Glasser, *The Quality School*, 76–78.

33. Crisis Prevention Training Institute, *Non-Violent Crisis Intervention: Training Program.* (Brookfield, Wisconsin, 1995), 8.

34. Robert E. Wubbolding, *Reality Therapy of the 21st Century* (Philadelphia: Brunner-Rutledge, 2000), 11.

35. Glasser, *The Quality School, 42–52.*

36. Eagle, T. L. and Snellgrove, Louis. Psychology Its Principles and Applications. 7th edition (New York: Harcourt Inc., 1979), 105?.

37. Glasser, The Quality School, 42-52.

38. Wubbolding, *Reality Therapy*, 18.

39. Good, *In Pursuit of Happiness, 37.*

40. Glasser, *The Quality School*, 57.

41. Ibid, 59.

42. Demartini, *The Heart of Love*, 40.

43. Ibid, 221–225.

44. Dake, J.A et al. "Teacher Perceptions and Practices Regarding Bullying Prevention." *School Health* 79: 9 (Nov 2003): 347–55.

45. Demartini, *The Heart of Love*, 32.

Appendix 1

Administration Guidelines for the Demartini Method

A. In columns 1 and 8, ensure there are an equal number of positive and negative traits.

B. In columns 2 and 9, ensure that the learner has identified sufficient people in his past, present, or anticipated future so that he has genuinely convinced himself that he has the same trait in similar or different forms to the same degree of quantity or quality.

C. In column 3, ensure the learner identifies a sufficient number of drawbacks to counterbalance her current perception of the positive trait in column 1 and in column 10 a sufficient number of benefits to counterbalance her current perception of the negative trait in column 8.

D. In columns 4, ensure that the learner identifies a sufficient number of drawbacks to others to counterbalance his current perception of the positive trait in column 1 and a sufficient number of benefits to others to counterbalance his current perception of the negative trait in column 8.

E. In columns 5 and 12, ensure that the learner identifies a sufficient number of people who perceive the opposite trait in the person.

F. In columns 6 and 13, ensure that the learner identifies how the perceived trait was exactly counterbalanced by its opposite trait by himself or others, one or many people, male or female and local or non-local at the same moment in time.

G. In columns 7 and 14, ensure the learner identifies a sufficient number of drawbacks and benefits, respectively to equilibrate her if she noticed the person displaying the opposite trait.

Appendix 2

The Purpose of Each Column of the Demartini Method

Each column serves a specific function and is related to other columns.

Side A

Column 1 serves to identify the positive trait we view as one-sided.

Column 2 serves to prove, first, that each of us have the positive traits we perceive in others. It is just that we have not noticed them while others have noticed them in us. While the form of the trait may differ and who sees it may differ, still each of us have the trait according to someone, sometime, somewhere. And if we really review our personal history we find that we have it to an equal degree as the person we perceive it in. Second, this realization creates an ownership of the trait and elevates a minimized self, i.e., builds self-confidence in the bullied. And third, it helps us learn the transparency of these traits, that others see them in us.

Column 3 dissolves infatuation with having the trait ourselves.

Column 4 dissolves arrogance with having the trait ourselves.

Column 5 dissolves perception-based labels and opens up communication.

Column 6 raises awareness of the laws of conservation and symmetry and humility before the laws of nature.

Column 7 dissolves the fearful nightmare of the person having the opposite negative trait.

Side B

Column 8 serves to identify the negative trait we view as one-sided.

Column 9 serves to prove first, that each of us has the negative traits we perceive in others; second, it helps us learn the transparency of these traits, which others see in us; and third, it de-elevates the maximized self, fostering humility in the bully.

Column 10 dissolves resentment with having the trait ourselves.

Column 11 dissolves guilt or shame with having the trait ourselves.

Column 12 dissolves perception-based labels and opens up communication.

Column 13 raises awareness of the laws of conservation and symmetry and of humility before the laws of nature.

Column 14 dissolves the elative fantasy of the person having the opposite positive trait.

Appendix 3

The Process of Accelerated Learning in the Demartini Method

As one proceeds through the columns it is vital that the learner find an equal **quantity or quality** in each column to restore an emotional balance. So each question's purpose is to assist and accelerate the creation of this awareness of the counterbalance within the learner's awareness:

In columns 1, the learner records a number of positive traits in the person. *Please note that traits can also be perceived as action or inactions of the person.*

In column 2, the learner learns they have the same positive trait in other forms to an equal degree.

In column 3, the learner learns there is an equal cost and benefit to having this positive trait.

In column 4, the learner learns there is as much cost as benefit to others who perceive the learner with this positive trait.

In column 5, the learner learns there are just as many other people who perceive this person with the opposite trait.

In column 6, the learner learns that the opposite trait was also being projected on her to an equal degree at the same moment in time in some form by either one or many people, either male or female, either locally or non-locally and either by herself or others.

In column 7, the learner learns that if the person displayed the opposite trait it would benefit them to an equal degree as the current trait they are noticing.

In the same way in column 8, the learner learns that there are an equal number of negative traits as identified in column 1 in the person.

In column 9 the learner learns that she has the same negative trait in other forms to an equal degree.

In column 10, the learner learns that there is an equal benefit and cost to having this negative trait.

In column 11, the learner learns there is as much benefit as cost to others who perceive the learner with this negative trait.

In column 12, the learner learns that there are just as many other people who perceive this person with the opposite trait.

In column 13, the learner learns that opposite trait was also being projected on her to an equal degree at the same moment in time in some form by either one or many people, either male or female, either locally or non-locally and either by herself or others.

In column 14, the learner learns that if the person displayed the opposite trait, it would cost them to an equal degree as the current trait they are noticing.

Appendix 4

The Intervener's "What's Next?" Technique

Having just completed reading *The Dance of Bullying … A Breakthrough Tool for Teachers and Parents,* you are likely quite interested in the content yet find yourself asking a very important question, "What else can I do to help the kids in my classroom work through the bullying dance?"

As educators and parents, we, like you, understand how important it is to have a concrete, practical process to assist with the implementation of concepts. To that end we offer you a simple and effective technique that can be used in three ways: first with the bully and the bullied individually; second, with the bully and the bullied together; third, it is an effective technique to use with the whole class, each of whom will have played the role of the bully, bullied or observer in some form. This technique will help raise the awareness of the group and equip them with new skills to work through bullying events as they arise. The technique consists of five simple questions that can assist any participant in the dance of bullying to move from the frustration or despair of a personal challenge to taking effective action to resolve it. This resolution most often comes in the form of new perceptions and new actions. This is contrary to most interventions since they generally repeat the same old behaviours and get the same old results. As an inspired Intervener, you can offer your students a new way of *seeing* by taking them for "A Walk in the Park." See figure 8.1.

Figure 8.1 A Walk In The Park

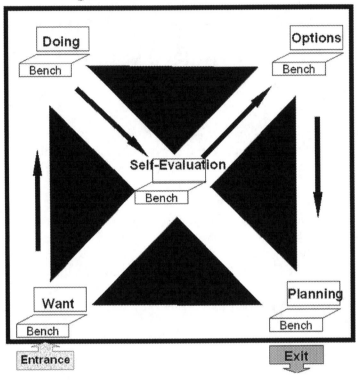

"A Walk in the Park" is a simple, practical, problem-solving tool learned easily and used quickly by an Intervener, be it a teacher or a parent. Its metaphor is a park similar to those many played in as children. This familiarity makes it an effective metaphor for use with struggling children and youth. By following the direction of the arrows and visiting each bench in the park and its corresponding question, the Intervener provides each child in the bully dance with an opportunity to explore their challenge with someone they already trust. The Intervener acts only as the guardian of a journey through the park. The bully, the bullied and/or the observer each have an opportunity to analyze their challenge with a supportive person who will encourage them to self-evaluate, balance their thinking and identify a new course of action.

Let us consider each question independently. Notice how each one facilitates the child taking control of his life and continuing to be a functioning member of the class, school and community. Each question comes from some aspect of

Choice Theory principles so there are no surprises in taking "A Walk in the Park." The five simple questions are:

1. What do you want?
2. What have you been doing to get it?
3. Has what you have been doing been working?
4. What else could you do to get what you want?
5. Are you ready to make a plan?

Each question corresponds to one of the benches in "A Walk in the Park." Let us consider each briefly and their role in assisting a child to work through their current challenge.

1. <u>What do you want?</u>—**Want Bench**

The Want Bench begins the journey through the park. As we stated in chapter five, every child (person) has a quality world or value system that provides the motivation for his behaviours—the source of his wants. When a child has a problem, this means that he perceives that some part of the real world does not match his quality world. In other words, he has a want that he does not know how to fill. *So underneath every complaint, criticism, blame, or frustration is a want.* It is important to help the child put that want into words, which can provide an understanding and direction for his future actions. This is the perfect place to start. Since he is being asked what he wants rather than what he doesn't want, it is not unusual for this to be the first time that the child has actually put what he wants into specific words. Of course, at all times in this journey the Intervener is careful to avoid any judgements of what the child wants. *This non-judgemental approach is crucial to the success of "A Walk in the Park."*

2. <u>What have you been doing to get it?</u>—**Doing Bench**

The Doing Bench is the next bench to visit because it helps the child to identify and appreciate all that he has been doing so far to deal with his challenge. It is often useful for the Intervener to have a way of recording or remembering each specific effort the child has already made to solve his problem so that they can be referred to later. It is here that the Intervener can acknowledge all the efforts already make by the child without judging the appropriateness of any of their actions.

3.   <u>Has what you have been doing been working?</u>—**Self-Evaluation Bench**

The Self-Evaluation Bench in the center of the park is next. This bench is in the centre because it is *crucial* to the effectives of "A Walk in the Park." It is here that the child gets to self-evaluate and let go of his earlier attempts to solve his problem while keeping his self-respect—one of our highest values. It is here that the child is asked to evaluate each and every of his earlier efforts. Since he self-evaluates without any judgement from his Intervener, he is able to let go of these choices and move on to find new options. This is the critical difference that makes the difference in the Choice Theory approach: *children learn best by self-evaluating.* The same principle is applied to their personal challenges as well as their academic work. Once a child has self-evaluated his earlier behaviour choices and heard himself say they did not work, it becomes difficult, if not impossible, for him to use them again in the current situation. This then frees his creativity to generate other possible options at the next bench. If someone else evaluates his behaviours, he feels attacked and is driven genetically to defend his actions in order to retain his self-respect or sense of power.

4.   <u>What else could you do to get what you want?</u>—**Options Bench**

The Options Bench is next on our walk. Now that the child is freed from his ties to his earlier attempts because he has decided through self-evaluation that they were ineffective, he is ready to use his own creativity to identify other possible options to move him toward his quality world and values. Since the quality world is not real, the Intervener is striving not to recreate the child's quality world, but rather to move him towards some aspect of it that is deemed important. Again, it is important that the Intervener record or remember all the possible options that the child generates. Strive for at least five to seven action options that he could take that would move him towards what he wants.

5.   <u>Are you ready to make a plan?</u>—**Planning Bench**

At the Planning Bench, the child selects one of his options from the previous bench that he believes will take him towards what he wants. It is vital that the choice be in the hands of the child so that the result is also his. This empowers him. It is important for the Intervener to emphasize to the child that, like all important things in life, his move towards what he wants will usually be achieved one small step at a time. The child selects the option and the Intervener then assists him to develop a specific and detailed plan of action that is likely to take him towards what he wants by responding to the specifics of:

- *What* exactly are you going to do?
- *Who* specifically does it involve?
- *When* specifically are you going to do it?
- *Where* are you going to do it?
- *How* are you going to do it?

There is no need to ask why the child will do the plan because the Intervener already knows that the *why* is because the child perceives that it will take him toward his quality world or values. This approach is quick, simple, and most importantly, it works. Let us look at a brief example to illustrate.

At school, Jason, an eighth-grade student, approached his teacher Mrs. Northrup, complaining that his homework is not completed because he cannot seem to focus on his work because he has so much going on. He added that besides his homework, he has to get ready for the upcoming hockey season and he seems to keep gaining weight, even though he has been avoiding junk food all summer. And to make matters even worse, Drew, one of his more popular team mates, has been ridiculing him verbally during practice, calling him names such as "fatty," "porky" and "hefty." He is frustrated, hurt and overwhelmed. He says he is ready to quit the team, but playing goalie is one of the things he loves the most and his grades are really important to him as well.

Mrs. Northrup has been Jason's teacher for over two months now and perceives him as a hard worker both in and out of school. She sees that he is very upset and so asks him if he would like to talk about it for a few minutes—to take "A Walk in the Park." Jason agrees because Mrs. Northrup is perceived as a caring and respected teacher by many of the kids and so he trusts her. Let's follow their conversation to see and hear how Mrs. Northrup guides Jason through "A Walk in the Park."

Remember the five simple questions are:

1. What do you want to happen?
2. What have you been doing to get it?
3. Has what you have been doing been working?
4. What else could you do to get what you want?
5. Are you ready to make a plan?

Using these five simple questions as his reference,

1.   <u>Mrs. Northrup takes Jason first to the Want Bench—What do you want?</u>

Mrs. Northrup says: Jason you sound pretty frustrated and discouraged about your health, your school work and the way Drew is treating you. What do you want out of this situation you find yourself in right now?

Jason responds: I want to be healthy and stay fit for sure and my grades are important to me so I want to do well on the tests coming up next week. But what is also bothering me a lot is Drew's name-calling. I want that to stop as well. I guess I want a lot of things.

Mrs. Northrup asks: Which one do you want first? Which do you want to move towards right away?

Jason: Well I guess that would be dealing with the way Drew is treating me. I really worry about it a lot and find myself eating to distract myself. It seems to interfere with both my focus on my fitness and my studies.

Mrs. Northrup clarifies: How do you want Drew to treat you, Jason, specifically?

Jason: I want him to treat me with respect like he does everyone else. I am our goalie and part of the team just like him.

Mrs. Northrup clarifies further to assist Jason to specify his wants: How would Drew have to behave toward you that would indicate to you that he was respecting you?

Jason: He wouldn't have to be my friend, but he could call me by my name instead of the names he has been using. He could listen to what I have to say during our post-game debriefs. He could congratulate me on a good game like the other players do.

Mrs. Northrup focuses Jason's attention on his highest priority: Of those three things, which is the most important to you, Jason?

Jason: If he would just call me by my name that would sure be a great beginning.

2. <u>Mrs. Northrup now moves Jason to the Doing Bench—What have you been doing to get it?</u>

Mrs. Northrup: Jason, I think that makes a lot of sense! So, what exactly have you been doing so far to get Drew to call you by your own name?

Jason: Well, as I mentioned, I have been worrying about it a lot. And once, I gave him a dirty look when he called me 'porky.' And for a while I have tried ignoring him. I also asked some of my friends if I should tell him off in front of everyone, but they didn't know what I should do. I have even considered fighting him, but I don't know if I could win or not.

3. <u>Mrs. Northrup takes him next to the Self-Evaluation Bench—Has what you have been doing been working?</u>

Mrs. Northrup says: Jason, you sound like you have been doing several things but I want to ask you a question about each of them. Think about your answer carefully. Has worrying about this situation got Drew to call you by your name?

Jason: Not really. And I have been wasting a lot of time as well.

Mrs. Northrup: Has giving Drew dirty looks got him to call you by your name?

Jason: Actually, I think it encourages him more, so no, it hasn't worked either.

Mrs. Northrup: Has ignoring Drew got him to call you by your name?

Jason: No, ignoring him hasn't worked either.

Mrs. Northrup: Jason, has talking to your friends about it got Drew to call you by your name?

Jason: Not really. They don't know what to do, and some seem glad that he is not picking on them.

Mrs. Northrup: Jason, do you think considering picking a fight with Drew, whether you won or not, would get him to call you by your name?

Jason: You know, when I think about it, if I won, he would probably just come and get me back with some of his friends, and if I lost, he would call me even more names, so no, I don't think it would get him to call me by my name either.

Mrs. Northrup: So, while these behaviours may have worked in other situations, they haven't been effective in getting Drew to call you by your name, is that true?

Jason: Yes, that's true.

4.   <u>Mrs. Northrup takes Jason next to the Options Bench—What else could you do to get what you want?</u>

Mrs. Northrup: Given that the things you have tried have not worked what else could you do to get Drew to call you by your name? I want you to just brainstorm options that you could consider and see what you come up with?

Jason: Well, let's see. I suppose I could call him names back, like 'skinny,' or 'bean pole' or 'stretch.' Also, I could make a joke about it like it was no big deal. And I guess I could just tell him straight-up that I am hurt and offended by what he says and that I wish he would call me by my name like I do him. And I could even remind him that we have a no-name-calling policy in our school and that if he continues it could affect him being on our team. And I could get my best friend Stan, who is really a big guy, to come with me to show Drew I am serious. And I could even just report what he's been doing to our team coach or even our school principal. You know, when I think about it carefully, there are a lot of things I could do about it. I didn't realize how many choices I have.

5.   <u>Mrs. Northrup takes him lastly to the Planning Bench—Are you ready to make a plan?</u>

Mrs. Northrup: Jason, you have created six new options that you could consider doing to move towards getting Drew to call you by your name. Which one are you ready to act on that would take you towards getting Drew to call you by your name?

Jason: Well, when I think about it now, I want him to respect me by calling me by my name, so if I disrespect him in any way it isn't likely to help much, so I think the best one for me at this point is the third one, telling him how I feel about the name calling. He may not stop but at least I will know that he knows how I feel about it.

Mrs. Northrup: Are you ready to make a specific plan around the option you have chosen, Jason?

Jason: Yes, I am!

Mrs. Northrup: Okay! What specifically are you going to do? When specifically are you going to do it? Where specifically are you going to do it? How specifically are you going to do it? And who specifically does it involve?

Jason: Well, what I am going to do is talk to him face-to-face and tell him how I feel about his calling me names. The 'when' will be after our next practice on Tuesday afternoon? The 'where' will be alone outside the rink? The 'how' will be that I will tell him that I am a valuable part of the team too, and I wouldn't treat one of my team mates this way, and when he does, I feel disrespected and hurt. And that I would appreciate it if he would call me by my name in the future. And the 'who' is just Drew and me.

Mrs. Northrup: Let's see how strongly you are committed to your plan, Jason. On a scale of one to 10 with 10 being the highest commitment, how strongly are you committed to it?

Jason: You know, Mrs. Northrup, just talking to you about it has helped me feel better and realize there are lots of things I can do to deal with this situation. I am really committed, at least an eight or a nine. I am much more confident now that I can deal with this situation.

Mrs. Northrup: Good for you, Jason. Will you let me know how it goes?

Jason: I sure will, Mrs. Northrup, and thanks for listening. I really appreciate it. You know, just talking it out has helped me realize that I am stronger and more self-confident than I realized and that there are lots of potential solutions to my challenges. And not just with Drew but also with my health and studies. In a funny sort of way, Drew has actually helped me gain more confidence in myself by giving me a hard time. Go figure!

<u>Note</u>: Regardless of the nature of the bullying problem, the process of guiding someone through "A Walk in the Park" does not change. *Use the same path to the same benches in the same order.*

<u>Notice</u>: Mrs. Northrup's role as Intervener is to serve as a guide on the journey, asking the relevant questions in her own words. Mrs. Northrup *does not judge, criticize, blame, complain, anger or threaten* Jason. Mrs. Northrup knows as an Intervener that Jason will find the answers to his own challenges using his own creativity, as long as she keeps him on the path to each bench in their prescribed order.

<u>Remember:</u> In the above scenario, if Mrs. Northrup perceives that Jason's challenge is not uncommon in the class or on the school teams or in the school as a whole, it might be advisable to use the same "Walk in the Park" process with groups of students within classes or teams.

Best wishes as you utilize this strategy with your students. You and they will achieve amazing results!

Appendix 5

The Dance of Bullying "Workbook" Learning Activities for the Classroom and Home

Chapter One
A New Approach

Life is not the way it is supposed to be; it is the way it is.
The way you cope with it is what makes the difference.

—Virginia Satir

Introduction

Bullying is a natural phenomenon that was and always will be a part of the human experience because it serves a useful function in the evolution of the social skill set of humans. By engaging students in these activities based on the scientific laws of symmetry and conservation, teachers can establish a simple and practical means of dealing with bullying in their learning environment.

These learning activities focus on the following points:

- There is a natural balance in all events and so an equal number of gains and losses.
- There can be no pain without pleasure or pleasure without pain in some form.
- We each have some form of all 4600 human traits.

Learning Activities

1. <u>Being Perceived as a Bully</u>

Ask the students to think about a time when they felt very confident but were perceived as arrogant, aggressive and/or disrespectful—in other words, a bully. Encourage individuals who argue, "I am never like that" to explore further.
   Then ask:

   a.   Who specifically perceived you as such?

   b.   How specifically were you behaving?

   c.   What specific feelings did you generate from being viewed this way?

   d.   What was the outcome?

Now ask your students to identify the gains and losses of the situation using each of the seven categories of life described in table 2.3. Check out chapter two and table 2.2 to get started.

2. <u>Being Perceived as Bullied!</u>

Ask your students to think of a time when they were not confident and may have been described as weak, fearful or inexperienced; in other words, bullied. Remind your students that since every human has all 4600 known traits, it is not possible to not display these traits in some form.
   Once the students have located the experiences ask them:

   a.   Who specifically perceived you as such?

   b.   How specifically were you behaving?

   c.   What specific feelings did you generate from being considered this way?

   d.   What was the outcome?

Now ask them again to identify the gains and losses of the situation using the seven categories of life in table 2.3 until they see the perfect equilibrium.

3. <u>The Great Discovery</u>

Preamble—Review with your students the laws of symmetry and conservation, explaining that every person will always be supported and challenged equally in every event, either by themselves or someone else, by one or many people, or by real or imagined people. Then ask your students to take a full page and make two columns on it, labelling the left column "Challengers" and the right column "Supporters."

Part A—Then ask your students to identify real events with family, friends, clubs and teams where they felt put down in some way.

- In the "Challengers" column, ask the students to list specific people they perceive put them down in each of these situations.

- Now ask the students to identify in the "Supporters" column those who, at the very same moment in time, were being supportive towards them or lifting them up. Was it themselves or someone else, one or many people, real or imagined people?

Part B—now reverse the role from being bullied to being a bully.

- Using the same two-column matrix again, ask your students to find a time when they put down another person. Ask them to put their own name in the "Supporters" column for each event.

- Then ask your students to identify who was challenging them at that very moment. Was it themselves or someone else, one or many people, real or imagined people?

- Remind them it will be to the same degree that they were putting the other person.

- Struggling to find the counterbalancing person(s) is common. Encourage your students to persist by offering personal examples. We as humans precisely follow the laws of symmetry and conservation, so it is not possible for there not to be an equal amount of positives and negatives in each interaction. Assist your students to see the laws of symmetry and conservation at work in every example they identify.

Chapter Two
When Were You Bullied?

The real voyage of discovery consists not in seeking new
landscapes but in having new eyes.?

—Marcel Provost

Introduction

Our beliefs are what we hold to be the truth about life. Our values are just a reflection of our belief system. We strive to live by our values and so make up rules to live by. Every event in our lives, including bullying and being bullied, contributes to our being who we are. We can often see how successes in our lives contribute to our growth, but it is less obvious to us that our failures contribute equally to our evolution. It is vital to honour *all* our experiences, to see both sides of every experience we encounter; otherwise, we are destined to repeat it until we do. This is often a leap in awareness, a leap in thinking, but it is a truth of the natural world.

Most people tend to focus their perceptions of what is lacking in life—voids—rather than taking on a perspective of abundance. Unfortunately and fortunately, this thinking contributes to our getting stuck in one place, i.e., revolving; but, it also contributes to driving us to new learning places, i.e., evolving. These voids, as they are perceived, serve as a catalyst to become a compelling force in our lives. In other words, they form our values or what is very important to us. How many people do you know who have "risen from the ashes" of their lives to achieve greatness and contribute significantly to the lives of others? You see, their perceived voids have become important values and serve as a catalyst for their inspiration and their destiny.

These learning activities focus on the following points:

- We each have all human traits and display them in some form.
- A perceived void from our past drives us to create an inspiring value.
- The laws of symmetry and conservation explain the value of bullying.

Learning Activities

1. <u>Collecting Your Evolutions</u>

Preamble—Ask your students to think back on their work in the chapter one activities and about being bullied and being a bully. Then ask them in random triads to discuss the following questions:

    a.   What have you learned about yourself?

    b.   What are the gains and losses of these experiences?

    c.   Do you see how you have every trait you love ***and*** despise, just in a different form?

    d.   What has been a "light bulb" moment?

    e.   Do you feel grateful for these experiences that helped you become wiser and more self-appreciative?

Then to complete the activity, ask them to create a list of the seven most important things they have learned to share with the class.

2. <u>The Rich and Famous</u>

Preamble—Ask each of your students to identify a famous person they admire, one who has contributed to society in a big way. Have them research and present on a poster board this person's life, noting particularly the following points:

    a.   the voids that became important values for this person

    b.   the symmetry or balance in their life story; the voids or challenges that fuelled their achievements and dreams which made their contributions possible

    c.   the 10 most admirable traits this person possesses and where they, the student, display these traits

    d.   who among their family, friends and classmates would say they display these same 10 traits

3. <u>The Symmetry Awareness Circle!</u>

Preamble—arrange your students in a large circle. Then ask them to think of a time when someone put them down. Ask them to describe that time to the group. Then ask each of them to demonstrate the laws of symmetry by finding and sharing with their group those who, at the very moment they were being put down, held them up or supported them. Ensure each person in the group gets a turn.

You may want to begin by volunteering to go first and offering a few example of your own.

Chapter Three
Where Do I Bully?

Our perception is our reality.

—John Demartini

Introduction

Whether bullying occurs is determined by the perception of the viewer and based on her own values. We believe what we need to believe to make sense of our experiences. Our values reflect what is most important to us from our belief system. So, we can trace the learning of every value to one or more perceived voids in our past.

Let's explore an example from Alice. Suppose my life experience included a strict and exact father. So, from my father I learned to believe that men in positions of authority are sometimes bullies and don't listen to my point of view. From that belief I concluded that it is important to listen to authority figures but also equally important to have a voice of your own. As a result, my response to his requests was to obey or experience the consequences. But in dealing with the consequence, I also learned the importance of standing up for myself. From this life experience I perceive a void of not being loved by my father in the way I wanted to be. But I equally learned to stand up for myself. The value that arose from this void assisted me in learning to stand up to authority figures and be authentic with myself and others, which I value highly.

These learning activities focus on the following points:

- We believe what we need to believe about ourselves and the world to make sense of our life experiences.

- Our values are determined by our belief system which is based on our life experiences.

- There are no perpetrators or victims in the bullying dance because each person gains and looses equally in the event.

Activities:

1. <u>Exploring Belief Systems</u>

Preamble—Ask your students to take a fresh page in their notebooks and follow your directions. Begin by explaining to them that we are born with an innate belief that we can be, do, or have anything we choose. This belief is often called our will to live or survive. The rest of our beliefs are learned mostly unconsciously from our experiences in our families, culture and communities. A belief is something you think is true for you, based on your life experiences so far. It may or may not be believed by anyone else. That will depend on their experiences. Beliefs are not permanent or tattoo-like; rather, they can and will be changed as we collect new experiences, which alter them and their related values.

Then ask each student to make a list of seven beliefs they have about a bully and seven beliefs they have about a bullied by completing the following statements:

I believe that a bully is _____.

I believe that a bullied is _____.

Once they have at least seven beliefs about each, assign them randomly to groups of three and ask them to share with their classmates their perspectives on the following questions:

    a.   How old were you when you learned these beliefs?

    b.   Where did this learning probably occur?

    c.   Who was involved in your learning these beliefs?

    d.   Have any of these beliefs changed as a result of recent learning?

2. <u>Exploring Being a Bully</u>

Ask the students to find a time in their life when they bullied another person. Then ask them to collect the following information on this event(s). (Example responses follow each item.)

    a.   Describe your specific behaviours toward the other person.
        I used words to bully a person.

    b.   What value motivated you to act this way?
        I valued having my opinion heard.

    c.   What void did you perceive in your life which generated this value?
        I did not feel accepted by my family or friends.

    d.   What value arose from this perceived void?
        It is important to listen to and appreciate people as they are.

    e.   Since nothing is ever missing due to the law of conservation (it is just in a different form), what was the unrecognized form of this perceived void?
        I realize my grandmother totally accepted me, just as I was.

Then to complete the activity, ask the students to share with the class their most important learning from this activity.

3.   Exploring Being a Bullied

Follow the same procedure as outlined in Exploring Being a Bully above, only this time use an example of when you perceived you were bullied.

    Ask the students to find a time in their life when they were bullied by another person. Then ask them to collect the following information on this event(s). (Example responses follow each item.)

    a.   Describe your specific behaviours toward the other person.
        I kept quiet and backed away.

    b.   What value motivated you to act this way?
        I valued my safety and my self-respect by avoiding embarrassment.

    c.   What void did you perceive in your life which generated this value?
        I felt weak and rejected with no friends.

    d.   What value arose from this perceived void?
        It is important to be strong and appreciate people.

    e.   Since nothing is ever missing due to the law of conservation (it is just in a different form), what was the unrecognized form of this perceived void?
        I realized I have strong family ties that are always there for me.

Then ask the students to share with the class how their voids and values are connected.

Chapter Four
The Dance of Bullying

*The great truths of nature cannot be arrived at merely
by close observation of the external world.*

—Albert Einstein

Introduction

As humans we cannot manage anything in which we cannot see a balance. And, yes, this includes bullying. We are actually perpetuating the dance of bullying by punishing the bully and rescuing the bullied.

Interestingly enough, both the bully and the bullied have psychological needs for power and belonging that drive their behaviours. The need for power and belonging are two of the four psychological needs that are innate and must be met daily. The ways we choose to meet these needs is through our behaviour. The behaviour we choose is our best attempt at the time to satisfy these needs.

These learning activities focus on the following points:

- The natural laws of symmetry and conservation apply to all human behaviour, including bullying.
- We cannot manage anything in which we cannot see the balance, including bullying.
- Our psychological needs of freedom, power, love and fun drive the behaviours of both the bully and the bullied.

Activities:

1. <u>Exploring Your Needs</u>

Preamble—Explain to the students that from choice theory we learned we have four psychological needs:

- **Freedom/Choice**
- **Power/Recognition**
- **Love/Belonging**
- **Fun/Progress**

Ask them to draw a large circle on their page. Then to divide it into four equal parts labelling each quadrant with one of the four psychological needs listed above. Now, using the seven areas of life listed below as a guide, ask the students to identify three behaviours in each quadrant that they use to meet these needs.

a) Spiritual (inner voice/vital spark)

b) Mental (self-appreciation/self-confidence/mental sharpness)

c) Vocational (school/education)

d) Financial (self-worth/managing resources/wealth)

e) Familial (connectedness/family relationships/harmony)

f) Social (friends/classmates)

g) Physical (energy/health/wellness)

Then assign your students to small random groups of five and ask them to share within their group one behaviour from each quadrant. Ask each group to identify the three most unique ways of getting one's needs met in their group.

2. The Dance of Bullying Meets Everyone's Needs

Ask your students to think of a time when they used bullying behaviours. Then have them identify how these behaviours met their four psychological needs. Ask them to draw a new circle and, using the same process as they did in the Exploring Your Needs activity above, write in each quadrant how their needs were served by this behaviour(s).

Now ask your students to do the same thing for a time when they used bullied behaviours. Then in random groups of five, ask them to identify at least three similarities between the bully and the bullied.

Complete this activity by leading them in a class discussion of how we all have the same needs regardless of age, gender, race or creed.

3. The Dance of Bullying—a Balanced Event

Preamble—Ask your students to draw on a sheet of paper the form Table 9.1— The Two Sides of the Two Sides. Using the information learned from the previous two activities in this chapter, ask the students, in new random groups, to complete this form, which focuses their attention on the two sides of the two sides of the dance of bullying.

Table 9.1 – The Two Sides of the Two Sides			
Bully		**Bullied**	
+ Gains +	- Losses -	+ Gains +	- Losses -

Remind the students to have a quantitative and qualitative symmetry and balance in their form, that is, an equal number in each column of the form and of equal importance across each row. If the student or group feels an imbalance, get them to keep filling in the column, adding additional rows if necessary, until they can see the inherent symmetry.

Then, to close this activity, when the form is completed ask each group to identify what value this activity might have for them in the future.

Chapter Five
The Art of Communication in the Dance of Bullying

As I am so I see.

—Ralph Waldo Emerson

Introduction

How well we communicate determines our ability to connect with others. Those skilled at communicating are aware of the power of their intent in the success or failure of communications. Many respected theorists build models of effective communication on intention. If, as many suggest, each person's behaviour is their best shot at a given time, then it is advantageous for us to better understand this powerful tool.

Intention is primarily delivered through how we say what we say. Intention includes tone, volume and cadence of speech. Emphasis placed carelessly, carefully or caringly can change the meaning of the same words and thus our intention.

We also learned that behaviour is more than an action; it actually consists of four components. We have the doing and thinking components and the feeling and physiology components. What we do and how we think actually generates and controls our feeling and our physiology. In fact, how we think is the most important influencer of our lives. Furthermore how we think (See figures 5.6 and 5.7 in chapter five) comes in two levels: first, how we think about the situation we are in; and second, how we think about ourselves in that situation.

According to Demartini, careless, careful and caring communications are choices we make as we communicate with others. You will recall earlier we said that *careless communication* happens when we disregard the values of others while imposing our values on them. The message is loud and clear: we will do it my way or not at all. *Careful communication* happens when a person surrenders his values and makes other people's values more important. This person is indecisive and has a big desire to please others, often at the expense of self. *Caring communication* happens when a person honours the values of another while honouring her own at the same time. This contributes to a state of graceful communication, a state of balance for both individuals.

These learning activities focus on the following points:

- The tone, volume and cadence of speech influence the meaning or intention of communications.
- All behaviour has four parts, with the doing and the thinking parts generating the feeling and physiological parts.
- The bully uses careless communication; the bullied, careful communications; and the wise educator, caring communications to intervene effectively in such events.

Learning Activities

1. The 55 per cent Law of Communication

Preamble—there is an accepted paradigm in communications that 55 per cent of the information conveyed is by body language. Explain to your students how you want to explore this idea with them.

    a. Before your class take six small pieces of paper and write down one statement on each. Make three positive or complementary toward the reader and three negative or derogatory from the list below:

- You are a smart person!
- You are good looking!
- You are a good student!
- You are a nerd!
- You are stupid!
- You are ugly!

Then fold each statement and place in a small container.

    b. Then ask for six volunteers to come to the front of the class to participate in an observation experiment. Explain there is a statement on each piece of paper you want them to read silently. Ask each student to select one at random.

    c. One by one ask each student in turn to read their individual statement to themselves silently and to imagine that they believed the statement to be true for a moment or two, even if they don't.

d. Ask the rest of the class is to note any change in each reader's physiology, such as facial expression, eye movements, body movements, etc. Give them a few minutes to write their observations before the next person reads his/her statement.

e. When each person has read their statement, discuss the group's observations about each reader's non-verbal communications during and after reading their statement.

Questions for the six readers:

*   What were you saying to yourself about the situation as you read you statement?

*   What were you saying to yourself about you being in this situation?

*   What feelings did you generate with these two levels of thinking?

*   What sensations did you generate in your body, such as: an altered breathing rate or heart rate, a tightening or restriction in certain muscles, butterflies in your stomach, a headache, etc.?

Questions for the observers:

*   What were you saying to yourself about the situation as you observed?

*   What were you saying to yourself about your not volunteering?

*   What feelings did you generate with these two levels of thinking?

*   What sensations did you generate in your body such as: a more relaxed breathing rate or heart rate, a softening of certain muscles, a calm stomach, etc.?

*   What did you notice about the way your classmates were responding to what they were reading from a physiological viewpoint?

f. Complete the activity by asking what they learned from this activity that could help in a bullying situation in the future. Remind them that words, even when they are not true, can have a profound effect on another person and therefore it is important we choose them with care.

2. The Influence of our Voice

Preamble—put each statement in the list below on a folded piece of paper and in a container. Divide the students into random groups of three. Have each group select two statements randomly from the container. Have each group take turns practicing the use of *tone, volume* and *cadence* of speech to convey an intention of both a complement and an insult. Then, after they have practiced and are able to verbalize each of their statements either as a complement or an insult just through tone, volume and cadence, have them exchange statements with another group to broaden the scope and depth of their learning.

- You are some cool!
- Do you always act that way?
- Like, what is your problem?
- Get a life, eh?
- You're awesome!
- Do you get out often?
- Did your mother dress you?
- Loan me five dollars?
- Give me your homework!
- Shut up!

Complete this activity by leading the class in a discussion of their most significant learning from participating in this activity. Ensure that each class member gets a chance to voice their perspective.

3. Self-Control is Paramount

Preamble—Review with your students the four components of total behaviour. Pay particular attention to the two levels of thinking, i.e., what you are thinking about the situation you are in and what you are thinking about yourself being in that situation.

Ask for four volunteers, one for each wheel of a car, each wheel a component of total behaviour. Ask them to form a rectangle facing the class, each sitting on a chair, at the front of the room. The students who represent doing and thinking sit on the front chairs and the other two students, representing feeling and physiology, sit behind them in the other two chairs.

a. For the First Phase of this activity, ask students to imagine being in a classroom where they are about to write a test. They have read through the questions and begin to write with ease because they know they know all the answers.

b. Then guide the students who are sitting on the doing and thinking chairs through the process.

c. For the student on the doing chair, inquire about what they would be doing with their body by offering an example, such as: starting to answer the first question, writing out its answer, etc.

d. For the student on the thinking chair, inquire about what they would be thinking, both about writing the test and about themselves writing the test by offering examples, such as: "I will do well on this test!" or "I am smart to have studied for this one!"

Now move to the feeling and physiology chairs behind them.

e. For the student sitting on the feeling chair, ask him how he would be feeling if he knew the answers and was thinking he would do well on the test and that he was smart. Offer suggestions to assist if necessary, such as: "good," "excited" or "proud."

f. For the student sitting on the physiology chair, ask her what would happen inside her body to her breathing rate, her heart rate or her muscle tension level if she was feeling "good," "excited" or "proud." Again, use the previous student's language whenever possible.

For the <u>Second Phase</u>, look at the opposite situation of knowing little or nothing on the test. Then beginning at the first chair, the doing chair, repeat the process again and note the differences in what goes on at each chair.

For the <u>Third Phase</u>, divide the students into random teams of five and have them direct themselves through one of their favourite hobbies and then one of the chores they hate the most.

In completing the activity, ask the students to write down three places in their lives where their doing and thinking has impacted their lives without them being aware of it until now. Discuss their results as a class under the theme, "What we think about we bring about."

Chapter Six
The Demartini Method

We can only change our lives and create a world of our own if we
first understand how such a world is constructed, how it works
and the rules of the game.

—Michael E. Gerber

Introduction

Digging beneath the surface level of our awareness requires persistence and dedication. It brings to one's awareness the fact that every trait we admire in others
we have equally but it has a cost. Conversely, due to the law of symmetry, every
trait we despise in others we also have equally and it has a benefit. Then it starts
to dawn on us that all 4600 traits are merely tools we use to raise our levels of self-
awareness and self-appreciation.

You have explored the law of conservation, which states that nothing is ever
missing; we just need to find the current form of it. You saw the law of symmetry
at play as you discovered that you and every other person have experienced being
the bully and the bullied in some form. You also learned that "what you think
about, you bring about," or attract toward you, so you can discover its two sides
and its compliance with the symmetry law. You explored the influence of your
self-talk and the four parts of total behaviour.

In the last chapter, you learned about the power of intention: how you say what
you say. And furthermore, you have learned that caring communication enables
you to communicate your values within the values of another, thus creating a situation where you feel self–respect and respect for the other person. Caring communications reminds us to "seek first to understand then to be understood," which
can be restated as "seek to understand their values and then to be understood as
someone who respects one's own values, and theirs, as well."

These learning activities focus on the following points:

- The laws of symmetry and conservation are present in every event.
- Every trait we admire we have equally but it has a cost, while every trait
  we despise we also have equally and it has a benefit.
- The Demartini Method enables a person to uncover the symmetry in a
  bullying event and to move forward with their life.

Learning Activities

1. <u>Assertive vs. Aggressive Behaviour</u>

Preamble—Plan a coaching event for your students on the difference between assertive and aggressive behaviour. Explain to them that assertive behaviour has within it three distinctions from aggressive behaviour: first, respect for the other person; second, defined boundaries or limits; and third, a choice for the other person to opt out of the interaction.

   a. Assign them to random groups of five and have them flipchart a list of assertive behaviours and another list of aggressive behaviours.

   b. Then ask them to find the three differences that you mentioned above—respect, boundaries and choice—in the two lists. Ask them to cite examples of where they are present in assertive behaviours and absent in aggressive behaviours.

   c. Finally, ask them to identify where aggressive behaviours could be useful, such as to protect yourself or someone else's safety, and where assertive behaviours could be useful, such as when the other person perceives they are being disrespected in some way. Lead a class discussion on the implications of this in relation to how the perceiver is the final judge of his interactions with others.

   d. Ask the students in their groups to brainstorm seven examples of where they have been perceived as acting aggressive. Arrange for each group to practice changing an aggressive behaviour into an assertive one. Observe the groups and get one of the groups who have learned the difference to demo an example for the entire class.

   e. Engage the whole class with a new scenario. Walk around and listen to the mode of communication, the intention that is communicated; the tone, volume and cadence of speech; notice if the four parts of the total behaviour are congruent. Offer specific groups and students feedback to enhance their learning.

   f. Complete the activity by evaluating with the whole class's participation and offering them feedback. Then ask them to evaluate the experience and offer you feedback.

2.   Assertive vs. Passive Behaviour

Preamble—Use the same procedure as in Activity 1, Assertive vs. Aggressive Behaviour, but this time focus on the perspective of the bullied, passive child instead of the aggressive child.

So now plan a coaching event for your students on the difference between assertive and passive behaviour. Explain to them that assertive behaviour has within it the same three distinctions that passive behaviour does not: first, respect for the other person; second, defined boundaries or limits; and third, a choice for the other person to opt out of the interaction. Passive behaviour involves careful communication of disrespecting oneself, ignoring one's personal boundaries and giving away one's choices.

a.   Assign them to random groups of five and have them flipchart a list of assertive behaviours and another list of passive behaviours.

b.   Then ask them to find the three differences that you mentioned above—respect, boundaries and choice—in the two lists. Ask them to cite examples of where they are present in assertive behaviours and absent in passive behaviours.

c.   Finally, ask them to identify where passive behaviours could be useful, such as to protect yourself or someone else's safety, and where assertive behaviours could not, such as when the other person perceives they are being disrespected in some way. Lead a class discussion on the implications of this in relation to how the perceiver is the final judge of her interactions with others.

d.   Ask the students in their groups to brainstorm seven examples of where they have been perceived as acting passive. Arrange for each group to practice changing a passive behaviour into an assertive one. Observe the groups and get one of the groups who have learned the difference to demo an example for the entire class.

e.   Engage the whole class with a new scenario. Walk around; listen to the mode of communication, the intention that is communicated; the tone, volume and cadence of speech. Notice if the four parts of the total behaviour are congruent. Offer specific groups and students feedback to enhance their learning.

f.   Complete the activity also by evaluating with the whole class's participation and offering them feedback. Then ask them to evaluate this experience and offer you feedback as well.

3. <u>Total Behaviour of Communication</u>

Preamble—Review with your students the four components of total behaviour and then ask for three volunteers to demonstrate each component of a bullying behaviour and a bullied behaviour to the class from scenarios they have created.

Assist the students who are doing the demonstrations by asking them to share with the class each component in each of the two scenarios:

a. For the first bully scenario, ask the class to observe the tone, volume and cadence of words and body language. After the demonstration, ask the student volunteers to explain their awareness of their own components of their own total behaviour.

b. Repeat this same process for a bullied scenario.

c. Then repeat the process again, but this time demonstrating the total behaviour of a mutually-respectful caring communication between two people.

d. Complete this activity by asking your students to share the most valuable thing they learned from this activity.

Chapter Seven
Shall We Dance?

If we treat an individual as if he were what he ought to be;
he will become what he ought to be and could be.

—Johann Wolfgang von Goethe

Introduction

As an educator who understands the bully dance, you use presence, certainty and appreciation when intervening. You now know that bullying is a behaviour humans use in learning to satisfy our genetically-encoded needs. Furthermore, you know that the bullied, the bully and the observer are equally served by the event. And of special significance is the knowledge that if we refuse to learn from bullying we will unconsciously be drawn to other similar events until we learn the lesson of self-appreciation that bullying offers us.

These learning activities focus on the following points:

- Bullying is a tool or behaviour that humans use to satisfy genetically encoded needs.

- Nature treats events as *neither* right *nor* wrong, while humans treat events as right *or* wrong.

- If we refuse to learn the lessons that bullying events have to offer we will unconsciously be attracted to other similar events until we do.

Activities:

1. Every Trait Serves Us

Preamble—Prepare pairs of file cards each containing an opposite trait or behaviour. For example: dependent/independent, important/insignificant, assertive/passive, friendly/unfriendly, smart/stupid, etc. Ensure there is enough for each student to have one. Put a string on each card and randomly hang one card around each student's neck so the card hangs down their back and they cannot see the trait on their card.

    a. Instruct students to walk around for two or three minutes, reading the labels on the other students' backs, getting a sense of what each student's label means. Then signal them to start interacting with each other as if that person were the label he or she is wearing on his or her back.

Remind them that there is to be no physical touching or yelling but it is important that they use words and behaviours that will help the person guess the label he or she is wearing.

For example: If someone came up to me wearing the word "dependent," I might say, "I don't have time to work with you now, it would take too long. You're just too needy for me."

    b.   Then, after a few minutes of interactions, ask the students to guess their traits. They can help each other guess their labels, but encourage them not to give up too soon. Also encourage them to be aware of their own and the other students' total behaviours.

- What were they thinking while they explored the way people treated them based on the label?

- When they learned of their own label, what was their self-talk?

- How did it feel to be labelled in one way or another?

- Who was aware of some of the physiology attached to their label?

    c.   Ask the students to pair up with their opposite label and find at least three places where in the past or present they have utilized this trait. Find at least three ways this trait has served them. Then have them find at least three ways this trait has been a disservice to them. Encourage them to help their partner to do the same thing with his/her traits.

In closing this activity, ask the students if they can see that both their trait and its opposite serve them equally and that without the events in their lives where they demonstrated these traits, they could not, would not, be the unique and wonderful people they are.

2. Let's Dramatize Our Learning

Preamble—Assign your students to random teams of seven students. Have each group pick one of the five topics below and plan a skit or short play based on their learning about bullying. Ask them to ensure that their skit demonstrates some aspect of these learning points:

- Bullying is a tool or behaviour that humans use to satisfy their genetically encoded needs.

- The bully, the bullied and the observer are all equally served by this event.

- Nature neither treats events as right *and* wrong or *neither* right *nor* wrong, while humans treat events as right *or* wrong.

- There are two components to our thinking: what we think about the event and what we think of ourselves in the event.

- If we refuse to learn the lessons that bullying events have to offer, we will unconsciously be drawn to other similar events until we learn the lesson of self-appreciation.

As a follow up, your class may be interested in taking the live show to classes within your school and to schools within your area if they wish to share the message. Or perhaps they might even make a DVD to further share their wisdom.

3.   The Dance of Bullying

Preamble—Take your students to the gym. Bring a tape recorder or boom box with music that has a strong rhythm, a CD that is a favourite of the students will work most effectively.

a.   Play the music and encourage the students to find a partner and dance together to the rhythm of the music in some coordinated manner.

b.   Then ask them to change partners on your signal and repeat this until they have each had several partners in the dance.

c.   Then stop the music and gather them around for a discussion.

Ask them if they ever wondered why we dance. Explain to them that our entire being is filled with rhythms, from subatomic vibrating atoms to the beat of our heart and the rhythms of our lungs. Some research suggests that music is registered in the human brain as pure pleasure. So, dancing is a way to explore a variety of rhythms as a full-body experience. And this is what makes the music so intriguing. Ask them to notice what makes some rhythm a dance, like the waltz, for example. Generally it will be because the musical notes, the pattern of vibrations, the special steps and even the pauses all challenge us to coordinate our body movements to them while maintaining balance. Notice the various repetitive actions of our body that we use—back and forth, up, down and sideways—all synchronized within ourselves and with our partner. This challenge takes on a rhythm of its own and engages us in a fun-filled, beautiful experience, the music of the dance.

Ask your students to start noticing the rhythms of other parts of their life, other relationships in which they are involved. Ask them to notice from these experiences how, as their awareness of caring communication changed; their own rhythm did as well. And, ask them to notice how using the Demartini Method enables them to treat classmates as equals instead of placing them in a pit or on a pedestal. Through this new awareness, this self-appreciation and appreciation of others, their lives will become more balanced. This is the beauty of *The Dance of Bullying ... A Breakthrough Tool for Teachers and Parents.*

   d.   In closing, you may want to present your students with a certificate indicating they have participated in this work entitled *The Dance of Bullying ... A Breakthrough Tool for Teachers and Parents.* Create one for your students congratulating them as their facilitator and teacher.

   e.   Following the presentation of certificate, why not have some refreshments and encourage the dance in the gym to continue? Perhaps you and some of the other teachers and students may like to join in!

Chapter Eight
For Parents

Making a decision to have a child; it's momentous.
It is to decide forever to have your heart go walking around
outside your own body.

—Elizabeth Stone

Introduction

As parents of a child, you are their first and most important teacher. It is at your knee they first learn to walk, talk and make sense of their world. It is at your knee that they learn the beliefs and values that guide their future. Your role in their development is crucial. We know that social and emotional development influences cognitive and physical development. Emotions are simply a measure of a person's current ability to meet their needs. Emotions are just learning tools. Emotions are actually harmless until we express them in some way that is perceived as detrimental to ourselves or others. So, negative and positive emotions both create opportunities for parents and teachers to help children understand their feelings and to learn new ways to express them. Negative emotions tend to receive the most attention because they are perceived more often as violating our social mores. It is often a challenge for parents and teachers to deal with negative feelings in an effective way.

By acknowledging and labelling positive and negative feelings, children develop awareness of what makes them feel good and bad and how to create such feelings in themselves. Children often need guidance in channelling both positive and negative feelings. For example, when a child is highly excited he may exhibit highly rambunctious behaviour that can put another child at risk. Recognizing how what they do can affect others is important for children to learn. Reading others' reactions to their emotions can guide children toward using new ways to express themselves.[48]

As parents, we discovered that really loving our children meant supporting *and* challenging them equally, not one or the other exclusively. We learned that using caring communications helped our children know that we really listened to what was important to them, even though we didn't always comply with their wishes. Does that mean they sailed through life without difficulties? Of course they didn't; nobody does, and that would be a violation of the universal laws of symmetry and conservation. However, we are confident in the knowledge they have the skills to work through whatever crosses their path.

In our work with children and parents spanning 35 years we have not once encountered a parent who did not love her child. We have, however, encountered many parents who were frustrated with their children's behaviour and who needed words of encouragement and new strategies to help them meet with the demands of raising their children.

In addition to the suggestions listed at the end of chapter eight, we offer the following thoughts for your consideration as you support and challenge your child's evolutionary development:

1. Remember that your home is the child's first and most important learning environment, so every activity in this *The Dance of Bullying ... A Breakthrough Tool for Teachers and Parents* workbook is equally applicable at home.

2. Learn and practice caring communication in your interactions with your child.

3. In using caring communication it is important to know that guiding children's behaviour has three core components:

    *   Respect the child's feelings and values.

    *   Assist the child to find a new behaviour.

    *   Support and challenge the child to utilize this new behaviour.

4. Ensure your child sees, hears, sees and feels regularly the following messages:

    *   I love you no matter what you have done or not done.

    *   You are worthy of love no matter what you have done or not done.

    *   I believe in you, your genius and your potential.

5. Keep all rules simple, reasonable and achievable.

6. Model and teach your children how to think by:

    *   Listening to them

    *   Sharing your stories, wisdom and perspectives

    *   Challenging them to explore their innate creativity

    *   Encouraging them to solve their own problems

    *   Helping them look at options and consequences, both positive and negative

7. Since children learn what they live, model the values you wish your children to learn.

8. Create an environment where children experience opportunities to feel free to make choices, to feel powerful in making a difference, to feel loved, to belong, to have fun and to progress in ways that honour their values.

9. Respect your children for who they are and honour them just as they are. Support and challenge them to recognize and honour their own uniqueness.

10. Finally, we cannot over emphasize that you trust your own instincts, your own intuitive sense of what is appropriate for your own child. Children will offer you lots of continuous feedback. If things just don't feel right for you and your family, trust your "inner knowing." If you're uneasy about your child's behaviour, seek professional guidance from your child's teacher, a guidance councillor, a therapist, or a psychologist. And, remember *every helping professional is operating from within his own value system and experiences*, so feel free to check around until you find the right person for you and your child.

Resources

The following is a list of relevant resources that are available to explore the ideas, techniques and tools mentioned in *The Dance of Bullying ... A Breakthrough Tool for Teachers and Parents.*

a designed destiny inc.

The Dance of Bullying website
www.thedanceofbullying.com

Clarendon Consulting Logo

Clarendon Consulting
Kenneth L. Pierce
44 Grafton St.
Charlottetown, PE
C1A 1K5 Canada
Phone: (902) 569-3710
Toll Free: 1-877-569-3710
Fax: (902) 569-5433
E mail: ken@clarendonconsulting.com
Website: www.clarendonconsulting.com

<u>Taylor Consulting</u>
Alice M. Taylor
176 Lantern Hill
North Rustico, PE
C1A 1X0
Phone: (902) 963-2882
Toll Free: 1-866-963-2882
E-mail: a.taylor@pei.sympatico.ca

<u>The Concourse of Wisdom School, Houston Texas</u>
2800 Post Oak Blvd, Suite 5250
Houston, TX 77056 USA
Phone: (713) 850-1234
Toll Free: 888-DEMARTINI
Fax: (713) 850-9239
E-mail: info@drdemartini.com
Website: www.drdemartini.com

<u>The William Glasser Institute</u>,
22024 Lassen Street, Suite 118,
Chatsworth, CA 91311 USA
Phone: (800) 899-0688
Toll Free: (818) 700-8000;
Fax: (818) 700-0555;
E-mail: wginst@wglasser.com
Website: www.wglasser.com

Bibliography

Aczel, Amir D., *God's Equation: Einstein, Relativity, and the Expanding Universe.* New York: Delta Publishing, 1999.

Alcaraz, Roxie. *Fact Sheet—Bullying in Schools.* Riverside, CA: Centre of Excellence on Youth Violence Prevention, University of California, Fall, 2004.

Atkins, Peter. *Galileo's Finger: The Ten Great Ideas of Science.* New York: Oxford University Press, 2003.

Bauman, S. and C. Hurley. "Teachers' Attitudes and Beliefs about Bullying: Two Exploratory Studies." *Journal of School Violence* 4:3 (Oct 2005): 49–61.

Becker, Robert O. and Gary Selden. *The Body Electric: Electromagnetism and the Foundation of Life.* New York: Morrow, 1985.

Bryson, Bill. *A Short History of Nearly Everything.* Toronto: Doubleday of Canada, 2003.

Crisis Prevention Institute, Inc. *Non-Violent Crisis Intervention: Training Program.* Brookfield, Wisconsin, 1995.

Craig, W. M., R. D. Peters and R. Konarski. *Bullying and Victimization Among Canadian School Children.* Human Resource Development Canada Applied Research Branch Strategic Policy, n.d.

Crease, Robert P. *The Prism and the Pendulum: The Ten Most Beautiful Experiments in Science.* New York, Random House, 2004.

Dake, J.A and others. "Teacher Perceptions and Practices Regarding Bullying Prevention." *School Health* 79: 9 (Nov 2003): 347–55.

Demartini, John F. *The Breakthrough Experience.* Carlsbad, CA: Hay House Inc., 2003.

_____ *Demartini Seminars: The Breakthrough Experience (Seminar Manual).* Demartini Human Research and Education Foundation, Houston, Texas, 1988–2007.

_____ *The Heart of Love: How to Go Beyond Fantasy to Find True Relationship Fulfilment.* Carlsbad, CA: Hay House, 2006.

_____. *Demartini Seminars: The Demartini Method (Training Manual) The Breakthrough Experience.* Demartini Human Research and Education Foundation, Texas, 1988–2007.

_____. *Count Your Blessings: The Healing Power of Gratitude and Love.* Carlsbad, CA: Hay House, Inc., 2006.

Eagle, T. L. and Snellgrove, Louis. Psychology Its Principles and Applications. 7th edition, New York, Harcourt Inc., 1979.

Feynman, Richard P. *Six Easy Pieces.* New York: Basic Books, 1995.

Ferris, Timothy. *Coming of Age in the Milky Way.* Toronto: Random House Canada, 1989.

Glasser, William. *The Quality School.* New York: HarperCollins Publishers, 1992.

Good, Perry. *In Pursuit of Happiness.* Chapel Hill, North Carolina, Newview Publications, 1987.

Greene, Brian. *The Elegant Universe: Superstrings, Hidden Dimensions, and the Quest for the Ultimate Theory.* Toronto: Random House of Canada, 1999.

Gribbin, John. *Stardust: The Cosmic Recycling of Stars, Planets and People.* Toronto, Penguin Books of Canada, 2000.

Johnson, L. *SVRC Briefing Paper: Bullying.* University of Arkansas Criminal Justice Institute National Centre for Rural Law Enforcement, 2001.

Kiefer, Heidi, Nancy Cohen and Bonnie Pape. *Handle With Care: Strategies for Promoting Mental Health of Young Children.* Toronto: Hincks-Delcrest Institute, 2007.

Lederman, Leon. M. and Christopher T. Hill. *Symmetry and the Beautiful Universe.* New York: Prometheus Books, 2004.

Lederman, Leon and Dick Teresi. *The God Particle: If The Universe Is The Answer, What Is The Question?* New York: Dell Publishing, 1993.

Lipton, Bruce. *The Biology of Belief: Unleashing the Power of Consciousness, Matter & Miracles.* Santa Rosa, California: Sparrowhawk Publications, 2005.

Olweus, Dan. *Aggression In the Schools: Bullies and Whipping Boys.* Washington: Hemisphere Publishing, 1978.

Pellegrini, A. D. and J. D. Long. "A Longitudinal Study of Bullying, Dominance, and Victimization During the Transition from Primary Through Secondary School." *British Journal of Developmental Psychology* 20: 2 (June 2002): 258–280.

Wilber, Ken. *No Boundary: Eastern and Western Approaches to Personal Growth.* Boston, Shambhala Publications, Inc., 2001.

_____. *Quantum Questions: Mystical Writings of the World's Greatest Physicists.* Boston: Shambhala Publications, Inc., 2001.

Wolinsky, Stephen. *Quantum Psychology.* Norfolk, Connecticut: Bramble Books, 1993.

_____. *Trances People Live: Healing Approaches in Quantum Psychology.* Falls Village, Connecticut: Bramble Books, 1991.

Wubbolding, Robert E. *Reality Therapy for the 21st Century.* Philadelphia: Brunner-Routledge, 2000.

About the Authors

Ken Pierce, a psychologist, has worked for 35 years in psychology, education and business coaching. Ken is an international speaker and author who holds Senior Faculty status in the William Glasser Institute of Los Angles and is an adjunct professor of psychology at the University of Prince Edward Island. As well, he is a Certified Trainer in Neuro-Linguistic Programming, DACUM Facilitation and a Certified Teacher with the Demartini Human Research and Education Foundation.

Ken has published in the areas of stress management, learning environments, occupational analysis, early childhood education, and currently a business publication entitled "Using Lead-Management on Purpose." Ken's client list includes: Aliant Telecom, The Atlantic Lottery Corporation, Revenue Canada, Farm Credit Canada, Connors Bros. Ltd., Veterans Affairs Canada and The RCMP.

Ken is on the forefront of personal development and change that inspires people to find their life purpose and to live it daily. His methods are dynamic and engaging, his work gifted and inspirational. He shows people how to bring clearer purpose to their work and their life. Ken's related interests include jogging, trauma counselling and building gravity stone walls.

Alice Taylor is an adult educator who has more than 30 years of teaching experience as an Early Childhood Educator and college instructor. Her educational background includes Early Childhood Education, Adult Education, Choice Theory and Reality Therapy, Neuro-Linguistic Programming and non-violent Crisis Intervention. Alice has been the recipient of several awards for teaching excellence and was awarded the Queens Jubilee Medal for her "outstanding work with children and families."

Alice has a gift for knowing how to connect with individuals exactly where they are, inspiring them to uncover their gifts and their talents and showing them how to manifest them in the real world. Her current work consists of group and individual consulting in the form of life coaching, seminars, keynotes and weekend retreats. She has a regular column in a local professional newsletter entitled "What Does Alice Say?"

Alice has had a lifetime fascination for why people do what they do. To this end, she is a student of the Demartini Human Research & Education Foundation, through which she is committed to study and embrace the universal laws as they connect mind, body and spirit with human growth and development. Thus, she is dedicated to helping people see the gifts that are theirs alone to give and encouraging them to live fully from the inside out. On a personal level Alice is a devoted mother and grandmother, an avid reader, a creative decorator and lover of long walks in nature.

Printed in the United States
by Baker & Taylor Publisher Services

Thousands of children avoid school each day for fear of being persecuted by their peers; countless more dread it for the same reason. This timely, insightful, and truly practical handbook shows parents, teachers, school administrators, and community leaders how to create healthier, safer schools and communities.

Based on the physics and psychology behind bullying, *The Dance of Bullying* explains the interpersonal dynamics that cause one child to harass another. Easy to understand and apply, the tools and techniques in this comprehensive guide include:

- The innovative "What's Next" intervention strategy
- The groundbreaking Demartini Method® to enhance a child's feelings of self-appreciation and gratitude
- Skill-enhancing tips for both educators and family members
- Invaluable insights into the minds of both the bully and the bullied
- Specific actions to help adults intervene decisively

By understanding the bullying dynamic, you will be able to intervene with far greater impact—and in a way that honors everyone involved. With your help, all children can emerge from these relationships with greater self-esteem and improved interpersonal skills. With *The Dance of Bullying*, you will be able to instigate significant changes in your school and community.

Kenneth Pierce, a board certified psychologist and educator, has worked for thirty years in education, psychology and organizational development. An international speaker and an author, Pierce is a senior faculty member at the William Glasser Institute, Los Angeles, and an adjunct professor at the University of Prince Edward Island and certified by the Demartini Human Research and Education Foundation, Houston.

Alice Taylor has more than thirty years of experience as an early childhood educator, college instructor and life coach. Taylor counts the Queens Jubilee medal among her many awards for teaching excellence and outstanding work with children and families.

U.S. $16.95

ISBN 978-0-595-45303-0

51695

iUniverse
Publisher's Choice

9 780595 453030

THE TESTING GROUND

P. S. MILLER